HEART & SOIL

THE REVOLUTIONARY GOOD OF GARDENS

DES KENNEDY

HARBOUR
PUBLISHING

Harbour Publishing Co. Ltd.
P.O. Box 219, Madeira Park, BC, VON 2H0
www.harbourpublishing.com

Front cover photograph of Des Kennedy by Boomer Jerritt
Edited by Carol Pope
Index by Stephen Ullstrom
Cover and text design by Carleton Wilson
Printed on 30% PCW recycled stock
Printed and bound in Canada

BRITISH COLUMBIA
ARTS COUNCIL
An agency of the Province of British Columbia

Canada Council   Conseil des Arts
for the Arts   du Canada

Harbour Publishing acknowledges financial support from the Government of
Canada through the Canada Book Fund and the Canada Council for the Arts,
and from the Province of British Columbia through the BC Arts Council and
the Book Publishing Tax Credit.

Cataloguing data available from Library and Archives Canada
ISBN 978-1-55017-632-2 (paper)
ISBN 978-1-55017-634-6 (ebook)

Mud on boots
Kooky grin on your face
Love in your heart
And the whole earth waiting
Grow for it!

CONTENTS

PREFACE

AS EDITOR OF *GardenWise* magazine for more than a decade, I enjoyed the distinct pleasure of receiving, with every issue, what can only be described as "garden literature" from the ever-eloquent Des Kennedy.

Just what is garden literature? For me, it's the examination of gardening within the wider context of human experience. The recognition that choosing to live the life of a gardener is essentially a political act, a dedication to values and principles entirely at odds with consumer culture. That gardening is a day-by-day reverence of the life flow of earth, of the harmony so vitally required for the survival of this planet.

And—true to the nature of all literature—this literature must be expressed richly and compellingly in language that seeds a garden of imagery. For me, there is no one who does so more poignantly than Des, author of eight highly acclaimed books and considered by the *Globe and Mail* to be "one of the best gardening writers in Canada."

Now as a garden-book editor, I am privileged to support Des in this compilation of heartfelt, often humorous, always thought-provoking reflections about life from the cornerstone of a garden—a collection that honours those who, like the author, have chosen to love a little piece of earth as their way of expressing a greater love for Earth.

Four decades ago—with his partner, Sandy—Des salvaged "a dispiriting miasma of logging slash and stumps" on Denman Island. Pushing back against the dictates of a throwaway society, the couple replanted the sanctuary of forest for native plants and creatures, raised their own food and built a homestead from the very sticks and stones that lay beneath their feet.

And while cultivating the land, Des fought for it, working over many years to enhance the community and environment of Denman Island, including his role as a founding director of a community land trust and his direct involvement in campaigns farther afield—from aboriginal rights to the struggles in both Strathcona Provincial Park and Clayoquot Sound.

Throughout this volume, Des's richly textured background—including stretches as a monk and a scholar—shines through his musings on the "near-magical properties" and healing powers of a garden. Yet his voice as always remains comfortingly down-to-earth. For as contemplative and far-reaching as his thoughts may be, he is not afraid to poke fun at himself. "Earth laughs in flowers," says Ralph Waldo Emerson, and Des—shortlisted three times for the Stephen Leacock Medal for Humour—laughs too. But whether it is at himself wielding a "delinquent pole pruner like a jousting knight his lance" or wheelbarrowing downhill in a slide of "terrifying beauty," he remains keenly aware of the importance of all those who literally have the earth in their hands.

This is a book that joyfully celebrates the resilience of both the garden and the gardener, that helps us to find our way forward in the championing of the environment that sustains us—and that finds genuine hopefulness for both ourselves and our planet in "the abiding strength of resurgent earth."

—CAROL POPE

INTRODUCTION

IT'S A DELICIOUS paradox really: that gardening, which may seem from a distance the mildest and most innocuous of activities, can be at heart a revolutionary act. But so it seems to me, as to various guerrilla and renegade gardeners loose upon the landscape. Revolutionary in the sense of precipitating a fundamental alteration of affairs, as well as the overthrow of tyranny. The notion conjures images of wild-eyed gardeners massed in their thousands, brandishing hoes and manure forks as they march up Parliament Hill to oust the scoundrels.

I wish. But, of course, that's not the gardener's way. The uprising that begins down among the roots and rhizomes is first of all a transformation of perception. Of how we see the earth, how it feels to our touch, of how showers and breezes and sunshine form the backdrop of our days. We are earthstruck people and that makes all the difference. Seeing the earth for what it is, we are moved to treat it, always, with affectionate attention. We may or may not choose to struggle directly against the forces of uglification and pollution and oppression, but our primary purpose is to go the next step, to help in the work—alongside artists, healers, mystics and others—of creating inspired environments and opportunities for enlightenment.

Up to our gumboots in that process, we come to realize that working with plants in the creation of beauty and the production of food is, in its most highly evolved forms, just what our beleaguered planet needs most urgently: an exercise in harmony. Harmony: the combining of parts, elements or related things, so as to form a consistent and orderly whole, likely to produce an esthetically pleasing effect.

Extracting genetic material from an Arctic flounder and embedding it in the genetic makeup of a strawberry in order to enhance the fruit's tolerance to cold is not an act of harmony. Consuming forty-five thousand fossil-fuel calories to produce a one-pound steak containing less than a thousand calories is not an act of harmony. Roundup Ready terminator seeds are, at their kernel, tiny packets of profound disharmony.

All of that's old hat to seasoned gardeners. We have moved beyond identifying and lamenting the problems associated with dominance-driven strategies like genetic engineering and chemical pesticides, not to mention the overarching issue of climate change. And there's where the true revolution begins: looking instead to develop strategies and solutions based on harmony with the natural world and the human community. That's our endgame, building communities aligned with nature's wisdom, places of true beauty, places that provide healthful and abundant food for everyone.

Components of that revolution, although perhaps not reported amid the deluge of mayhem in the daily news, are arising in many places and many people working all over the globe. And the coalescing of those efforts—encompassing farmer activists in Bangladesh and Kenya's greenbelt tree planters and community-garden participants helping to transform inner-city neighbourhoods and schools—the combining of these parts into a whole, begins to trace the outlines of a sublime and hopeful harmony.

It is a place of brilliant connectivity where we are intertwined within the human community as well as the natural world of which we are a part. Here we encounter a landscape seething with vital energies: trees, stones, springs, soil itself—all are fully alive and animated, possessed of something our ancestors identified as soul. And our inner landscape too is an element of that harmony. Our longings and memories, our dreams and fears, our love for the other, these too flow through us and into the good earth and into the food we harvest and share. All of it—the sowing of seed, the tending of plants, the harvesting of crops —holds the astonishing possibility of transforming our lives and our society.

A tad grandiose, you might be thinking, but no less an authority than Thomas Jefferson said much the same thing two centuries ago: "Cultivators of the earth are the most valuable citizens. They are the most vigorous, the most independent, the most virtuous, and they are tied to their country and wedded to its liberty and interests by the most lasting bands." Revolutionaries of the spirit, that's what true gardeners are, and if the world's to become a better place, they shall have some part in its transformation.

THE PIECES ASSEMBLED in this little book represent a decade's worth of reflecting on the unexpected gift I was somehow given: to have the freedom, good health, loving relationship and wherewithal to devote myself, among other adventures, to life in a garden. Early versions of a majority of the selections first appeared in my *Earth Words* column in *Garden Wise* magazine, and about a dozen others as articles in the *Globe and Mail*. Freed from the constraints of column inches, most have been expanded and amended. They do not constitute a training manual for transformative gardening, being in places insufficiently solemn, if not outright frivolous. But they do attempt to collectively reflect upon gardening as an active engagement of the human spirit with the natural world.

I am particularly indebted to my current editor and former *Garden-Wise* editor, Carol Pope, for her wise guidance over the years and for encouraging me to assemble these pieces into this volume.

IN THE BEGINNING

Green-Fingered Grannies and Ancient Gentlemen

THE FIRST SMALL hints that spring is icumen in—the sweet scent of sarcococca by the doorway on a sunny afternoon, the thrilling shoots of stinging nettles in a sheltered corner—reawaken a great illusion: that springtime is the childhood of the year, the beginning of new life, a time of freshness, beauty and innocence, leading to long seasons of growth and fruitfulness. Late autumn and winter are seen as the seasons of age, spring the time for the lusty young blood of youth.

Poets have been dining out on this metaphor for centuries and, poets being what they are, insisting that youth is not only the first of life's seasons, but also the best. "That age is best which is the first," wrote Elizabethan Robert Herrick, "when youth and blood are warmer." Victorian Edward Fitzgerald was still plucking the same lyre three centuries later: "Yet Ah, that Spring should vanish with the Rose! / That Youth's sweet-scented manuscript should close!"

Having already received a gold card from the government, and thereby taken a considerable leap into the wisdom of age, I'm more inclined than ever to take issue with this infernal glorification of vernal youth. It's certainly true that, like the garden in springtime, youth's a lot of bloody muddling around in the muck. Sure, it involves great hot rushes of enthusiasm, considerable dreaming of impossible dreams and much swooning over objects of affection that will soon enough prove themselves more appealing in imagination than in reality. Youth's sweet-scented manuscript, much like a gullible gardener's order form for springtime seeds, all too often turns out to be a work of romantic fantasy.

Here's the bold counter-stroke I'm prepared to propose: that spring is at its pith the great season of our elders. Any thoughtful sounding of spring's resonances confirms that this is so. Even the most poetical gardener would hesitate to characterize the first growth of spring as new birth. The emergence of annuals planted from seed (indoors and often far earlier than required) does have this quality of the entirely new, but it pales in significance compared with the real growth happening at this earliest time of the year, the wonderful earth-surge trembling all around us. This isn't birth, it's rebirth, a stirring of ancient forces. The exotic spathes of swamp lanterns, the primeval flowering stalks of petasites, the jubilant nubs of crocus and snowdrops emerging from frosty ground— these are not birthings, nor the noisy exuberances of youth; these are the reawakening of old friends we have known forever.

Our culture at large, devoted as it is to the frenzied movement of merchandise, is unabashed in its obsession with the new and the hip and the hot and the flash. Dizzy crowds mill for hours through shopping malls, seeking articles of transformation, greying oldsters search for the fountain of youth. The glitter of illusions and delusions may be tastefully gift-wrapped for any occasion. Nature knows better; the garden knows better. In its depths, the old is new again and spring is its season of renewal.

Gardening is above all else an experiential undertaking. The longer you stay at it, the more you come to appreciate its complexities and depths. The true gardening community, unlike market demographers in cheap suits, holds in highest regard its elders, those who have had their hands in earth for half a century or more. I'm thinking of many remarkable sexagenarians and octogenarians whose gardens I've been privileged to visit. Of all our green-fingered grannies and aunties and mums, and of some ancient gentlemen too.

I don't know quite why, but so many of them are tiny wee people with impish grins and sprightly energy. Their eyes seem to twinkle with mischief; the lines on their faces are the outlines of smiles. Their minds are sharp as new secateurs, their enthusiasm high and their spirits still willing even though the flesh may have weakened just a titch over time. Make no mistake: these are the children of Pan, the true sprites of spring.

Were I to select a plant to symbolize them, I should choose the winter aconite, *Eranthis*. These are among the very first flowers to show themselves at our place, earlier than snowdrops or snow crocus. Their bloom is a miniature golden orb held above the frigid soil on a Tudor-style ruff of ornately cut leaves. They grow from small tuberous roots planted shallow. A day or two of sunny weather will coax them into bloom and if the weather turns filthy again, they simply huddle within their enfolding leaves and wait for conditions to improve. They are survivors, tiny but tough as nails and, once established, spread persistently through favourable places in the garden. Their hardy perseverance, their cheerful radiance during times too challenging for most other spring bloomers—these are the very qualities we admire in our gardening veterans.

So, by all means, let's join the poets in celebrating the warm blood of youth, but do so at the appropriate moment, as during the softer charms of May. For the true spirit of spring, the abiding strength of resurgent earth, I say let's look to the more tenacious beauty of our elders.

Fiddling on the Roof

"GETTING A JUMP on spring" is a fixation with certain gardeners of unstable temperament. Great lengths are gone to and fantastic technologies applied—grow lamps, heaters, hot frames, cloches and acres of floating row cover—all in the name of cajoling a few scrawny plants out of the earth slightly earlier than nature herself intended. "Forcing" is the term generally applied, suggesting images of horticultural thugs threatening plants with violence if they don't cooperate.

But serendipity sometimes arranges a less aggressive approach to hastening spring's arrival—perhaps simply a sheltered niche beneath a south-facing wall where a Christmas rose or snow crocuses bloom while all else remains a dreary smear of late winter.

Thus it was—unexpectedly but gloriously—with the sod roof on our woodshed. One might not normally associate sod roofs with harbingers of spring and, truth to tell, our first stab at sod roofing was more a harbinger of disaster. A stout little timbered building about nine by six metres, the shed's located directly behind the house, connected by a covered walkway so that firewood can be fetched, or the composting privy visited, during winter without our getting drenched in the process. The pitch on the shed roof is rather slight, something like thirty or thirty-five degrees—not steep enough for cedar shakes but, we calculated, not too steep for a sod roof.

Never one to do things correctly if an inexpensive alternative is available, I first created a sod roof employing multiple layers of asphalt paper, salvaged metal roofing and plastic sheeting. It was an incontrovertible failure whose initial small leaks gradually swelled into cascading rivulets that completely undermined the raison d'être of a roof. Eventually I tore the whole woeful business off and started afresh. A builder friend advised that we use EPDM, the rubbery fabric sold in garden centres as pond liner. After pawning the silverware, we purchased a single piece large enough to cover the entire roof. Balanced precariously on top of a ladder, trying to push the whole roll up onto the roof, I was almost thrown backwards by its weight and dashed to the ground, which would have put a definitive end to both me and the project.

Eventually, with the aid of my helpful nephew Greg, we got the EPDM spread out and covered to a depth of about ten centimetres with the soil and sod I'd removed from the previous roof. Then came the practical problem, which arguably should have been addressed before starting, but wasn't: How does one prevent the entire works from sloughing down and off the roof? I consulted a roofing specialist. As is frequently the case with specialists, the fellow seemed incapable of thinking outside the box, the way we enlightened generalists so often do. His dismissive response plainly implied he thought me mad to be putting sod on a pitched roof. Undaunted, I devised a clever scheme of laying a row of old bricks along the edge of the roof, hoping, rather than knowing, that they would be sufficient to hold the soil once the November monsoons began. Miraculously, they were.

Having survived the engineering phase, we were now poised for artistry. Across the south-facing half of the roof we planted a variety of creeping sedums—the little *Sedum obtusatum* whose tiny, fat, succulent leaves turn bronze-red in summer; the yellow stonecrop, *S. reflexion,* that inveterate spreader with its showy summer lacework of tiny bright-yellow flowers; the white-flowering native *S. lanceolatum;* 'Dragon's Blood' sedum; and whatever else we had around.

Next, a planting of the more robust sempervivums, long recognized as worthy rooftop dwellers. Then several clumps of chives from the vegetable patch. A scattering of species tulips: *Tulipa linifolia, T. tarda* and *T. turkestanica.* Lastly, dozens and dozens of snow crocuses and Dutch hybrid crocuses. All of these are plants that will thrive in thin, poor soil, are aggressive enough to compete with wild grasses and can withstand extreme drought in summer.

It's the crocuses especially that give us our low-tech "jump on spring." Sheltered from freezing breezes by the house, raised above the cold earth and tilted toward the pale spring sun, the south-sloping roof becomes a jubilant tapestry of new grasses and brilliant crocus blooms weeks before most of the cold garden below has awakened.

The crocuses and a few of the tulips have held on over the years, while sedums, sempervivums and chives have flourished. Grape hyacinths, *Muscari,* have found their own way up onto the roof. The aggressive little gold-moss stonecrop, *Sedum acre* 'Aureum', has also fit in well, its froth of tiny yellow flowers spilling charmingly over the edge. By midsummer the whole sloping surface is a lacy cascade of yellow and white sedum blooms among golden grasses. Certain ground dwellers from one floor below are also finding their way up and over the edge of the roof. An 'Albertine' rose has proven very adept at scrambling across a back corner, her long arms putting down rootlets as they go. On the other back corner, a rampant honeysuckle smothers the rooftop with fragrant blossoms, a particularly welcome component with the privy immediately beneath. Two other roses, 'New Dawn' and 'Mme. Grégoire Staechelin', along with a *Clematis* 'Nelly Moser', have also gotten a bit of a rooftop toehold.

Some plants did not adapt—a 'Silver King' artemisia packed it in after a year, and several clumps of rose campion, *Lychnis coronaria,* decided they weren't really high-rise dwellers either. The little tufted blue fescue, *Festuca glauca,* which from its colonizing activities in stony spots below we'd imagined would adjust nicely, failed to acclimatize. But, all in all, unlike its unfortunate predecessor, the roof has been something of a minor triumph. The jewelled carpet of plantings, like a small patch of alpine meadow, is directly at eye level from the kitchen window and you could hardly wish for a more heart-lifting vista while washing the dishes.

Still, I do take to musing that the roof would be a perfect spot for a bank of solar panels—eminently desirable, although not entirely compatible with the current illusion of a wildflower meadow. Truth to tell, if we were to start over again with building a house from scratch, among the many things I'd do differently would be putting a sod roof over the whole thing, for temperature regulation as well as beauty. And with solar panels, of course. But, for the moment, we shall have to content ourselves with this modest sod roof on a shed and the simple pleasures it gives, as when the snow crocuses are laughing their colourful heads off at the jump they've gotten on spring.

Romantic Gleanings

AN UNUSUALLY COOL and moist spring on the coast might have prolonged the melancholia wrought by a very wet winter had it not been for spring bulbs and perennials exulting in the wet and cool conditions. The winter aconites, snowdrops and crocuses seemed to linger far longer than usual. Lines became hopelessly blurred among early-, mid- and late-flowering bulbs, so that we had crocuses still hanging around while hyacinths and narcissi were in their prime and the early tulips were already blooming. The ecumenical effect was a splendid show that compensated handsomely for seldom ever seeing the sun.

Plus, the time was right for pondering the myths and legends that attach to the flowers of spring, many of which originate in the fable-rich regions of the Mediterranean. It's fascinating how so many of these ancient tales concern loss, rejection and death—tragic narratives one wouldn't readily associate with the exuberance of spring.

Crocus is a classic example. Greek legend has it that the flower was named for Crocus, a beautiful youth of the plains who was consumed with unrequited love for Smilax, a shepherdess of the hills. The hapless youth pined away and died of a broken heart, whereupon the gods transformed him into the flower that bears his name.

Rooted in misogyny as it may be, this familiar theme of unrequited love, featuring a cold-hearted maiden and soft-headed swain, echoes an old Persian legend that tells of a young man smitten by a beauty who declined to reciprocate. She may have had her reasons, but being peripheral to the narrative arc, these went unrecorded. The snubbed lover fled to the desert to die a lonely death. As he languished in the wasteland, weeping for a love beyond his reach, each tear falling in the desert sand was transformed into a beautiful tulip in bloom.

The theme of tragic love is given a slightly more Hollywood spin in a tale about forget-me-nots. Here, the story is of two young lovers meandering together along a riverbank. The gallant youth takes to plucking forget-me-nots for a posy to give his beloved, but he accidentally tumbles into the torrent and is swept away. As he's being dragged under, he flings the posy onto the bank and cries out to her to "forget me not!" And, indeed, who could after a dating stunt like that?

A more upbeat version occurred "on a golden morning of the early world" when an angel spied a daughter of Earth sitting on a riverbank twining forget-me-nots in her hair. Enraptured, the angel beseeched the powers of heaven to allow the lovely earthling to accompany him into paradise. But the powers of heaven, working the angles as they usually do, would only grant the damsel immortality after she'd sown forget-me-nots in every corner of the world (something forget-me-nots don't really need all that much help with). Our girl set about the task, aided each evening by her doting angel. Eventually, the job completed, maiden and angel entered paradise together, since she had gained immortality "without tasting the bitterness of death."

Still, the bitterness of death remained a major theme in heavenly springtime goings-on. Consider poor Hyacinthus. This beautiful youth was loved by the sun god Apollo, and also by Zephyrus, the west wind. One fateful day when Hyacinthus and Apollo were playing quoits (a celestial version of pitching horseshoes), Apollo tossed his quoit and jealous Zephyrus blew on it so that the heavy disk struck Hyacinthus on the head, killing him. Grieving Apollo changed the drops of blood spilling from his dead friend into hyacinths, a flower that came to symbolize vegetation reborn after being scorched by the hot disc of the sun and the desiccating west wind.

It was lecherous Zephyrus, too, who caused the death of the fair nymph Anemone. Noticing her windy husband's infatuation with the young beauty, Zephyrus's jealous wife had the nymph driven into exile, where she died of a broken heart, her body becoming the windflower that returns to life at the onset of spring.

And, for a final tragic tale, we have poor Narcissus, who idled away his days gazing at the reflection of his own face in pools. Though he came to symbolize self-absorption and egotism, this was an unfair legacy since the poor fellow was consumed with his own reflection only because it so closely resembled the face of his lost sister. Nemesis, the god of vengeance, turned him into the flower we know, destined to stand forever peering down at an image of himself.

What's uncanny about all these old stories of springtime tragedy is how accurately they capture the sense of loss and unseasonal wistfulness one feels, even in a lingeringly cool and moist season, as successive waves of springtime flowers, like young love itself, flourish then so quickly fade away.

The Great Canadian Hoax

I'M GOING TO propose that spring is the least Canadian of seasons. Collectively, we Canucks peak in autumn with what poet Wilfred Campbell celebrated as "Miles and miles of crimson glories, / Autumn's wondrous fires ablaze." The melancholy of fall, its sense of brilliantly extinguished expectations, fits our national psyche. We're passably good at summer, able to savour its sweet berries and wild roses, to splash and cavort at the lake. But even here we lack a truly sybaritic streak, being persistently aware in summer of how bad the mosquitoes are this year and how swiftly the season passes. Winter is our real métier, our true superbia. Ice crystals of chilling brilliance, the Northern Lights shimmering over untracked drifts of snow.

But the subtle spells of spring hold less magic for us than they might, I think because rapture is not an essentially Canadian condition. Our native caution serves us well in not giving way to romantic confections about the sweetness of the season. Should the prairie farmer, facing another year of disastrous losses—courtesy of subsidy curtailments and clever new trade arrangements—be rejoicing that planting time's at hand? Should the homeless, having survived the rigours of another winter on the mean streets of a Canadian city, be doing cartwheels because the tulips are in bloom?

A proper savouring of the season requires a jaunty optimism that a rebirth of wonder is at hand. But that's a tough sell when you're menaced by the risk of flooding after breakup; the detritus of dirt, litter and dog feces deposited by melting snow; and the almost instantaneous arrival of mosquitoes and black flies. Small wonder we're less than ecstatic. Then you get caught up in some moronic "Spring Fling" at the local mall where you're exhorted to "spring into the season" by cleaning up the yard, painting the house or generally exerting yourself in ways you'd rather not. Ah, for the dark comforts of January, when you could lie dormant without remorse.

No, springtime in Paris is not the same thing at all as the thaw in Moose Jaw. Who among our poets has been inclined to sing, "Oh, to be in Ontario now that April's here!" And even if you did genuinely thrill to the season, the damn thing's over quicker than a Hollywood marriage. The Calgary chinook's the epitome of the Canadian spring: from numbing cold to subtropical heat in a single afternoon. It's like a pubescent sexual encounter: months of panting anticipation climaxing in a five-second gush. Suddenly that's summer.

I believe our ambivalence toward the free-spiritedness of spring accounts for why virtually all our political leaders are such grey characters—pinched and parsimonious, the cronies of winter. Is there ever so much as a hint of spring's insouciance at a First Ministers conference? Even posing for the ritual photo in their casual slacks and sweaters, they're a dour and storm-door bunch. And that's how we want them to be; that's why we elect them. We did the other thing once, with Pierre and Margaret. A blood-red rose in the teeth, and all that. We let ourselves be springtime silly; we dared to hope and dream, to look about with laughter in our eyes—and you see where that got us. We'd prefer not to make April fools of ourselves that way again. Rather than risk disillusionment, we'll stick with this dreary pack of plodders, trudging the wastelands of fiscal prudence, with T.S. Eliot grumbling about how "April is the cruellest month," because it suggests a resurrection that we'd really rather not risk.

Except in British Columbia, where we're inclined to elect eccentrics to high office. At least some of the time, we like our politicians with a pinch of the wild riot of spring in them. These generally are in and out of office faster than a March hare. And that's because BC—at least coastal BC—breaks from the rest of the nation in its experience of spring. Here the season begins around the end of January and concludes sometime in late June. While the rest of the country's still locked in permafrost, the coast exults in an eruption of blossoms, and later on, while everyone else is roasting in summer sunshine, we're still tramping through the foggy dew.

Some residents—generally recent arrivals from points east—take to unseemly preening at this time, but the wise or wizened among us do not. We know the perils of life in perpetual spring, the whirling topsy-turviness of luteinizing hormones run amok, the recklessness of the heart and of pulsing blood. Dynamic and exciting surely, but a bit alarming and thoroughly un-Canadian, providing a cautionary tale to the more sensible rest of the country.

But then, inevitably, preposterously, spring breaks across the whole nation. Everywhere, people burst outdoors, rhapsodizing over the scent of lilacs or hyacinths, forgetting our customary circumspection, abandoning the First Ministers to their fiscal retentiveness, euphoric as raw life explodes all around us and our wary ambivalence is at last swept away in the delirium of spring.

It's Showtime

HORTICULTURAL TRENDINESS IS not something I have a whole lot of time for, but it is fascinating to observe how various enthusiasms ebb and flow through the world of gardening. Back in the 1970s when we started growing on Denman Island, it was all about food. Back to the Land, Self-Sufficiency, Grow Your Own—we were rich in slogans, even if not in topsoil. *Harrowsmith* magazine and *The Whole Earth Catalog* were our guiding texts. Mocked at the time as addle-headed idealists, we "new pioneers" had a fundamentally sensible ambition: to live and eat healthily by cultivating our own organic fruits, vegetables and livestock.

At a certain point—for Sandy and me it was in the late eighties—the lure of ornamental gardening began elbowing its way into the process. The island's big vegetable plots became complemented—in extreme cases, usurped—by equally ambitious rose arbours and perennial beds. Shortly thereafter, a mania for ornamental landscaping swept across the culture, as it does every few decades. Lawns and tennis courts were torn up and swimming pools filled in to provide space for dreamy plantings. Throughout the nineties, glossy new gardening magazines were launched, the number and size of garden clubs grew exponentially, specialty nurseries abounded, gardening television programs were inescapable and the gardening sections in bookstores threatened to push mere literature out the back door.

Plus, flower and garden shows—from the modest to the monumental—were mounted in many communities. Ever the opportunist, I became a regular at several of them, learning to appreciate in the process how these extravaganzas could get us jump-started midway through what otherwise might have been a decent period of hibernation.

The Northwest Flower and Garden Show in Seattle has, over its twenty-six years, grown into the third-largest such show in the United States. It's mounted in early February, and invariably packed with enthusiasts from all over the region. But for a really startling contrast between stark winter outside and blooming gardens within, no West Coast show could compete with Canada Blooms, the humongous flower and garden festival held in March, when Toronto can be at its least appealing. Back in the day, the festival was housed in the cavernous Metro Toronto Convention Centre and soon became one of the major garden shows in North America, attracting well over a hundred thousand visitors during its five-day run. The opening-night gala was a glittering affair adorned with divas, danseuses and the horticultural who's who of Upper Canada.

As befits the Big Smoke, everything was big at Canada Blooms—six acres of feature gardens, over a hundred entries in the floral-design competition, and sufficient lectures and demonstrations to earn one a PhD in horticulture. With abundant room, the festival gardens—high on forced bulbs, hardscapes and artistic extravagances—could be lingered over and savoured at a leisurely pace with none of the crowding and jostling that might plague smaller indoor shows. Participants who actually enjoy the ebb and flow of compressed humanity could squeeze into the market area where over two hundred vendors offered plants and accessories. While much of the show was necessarily Toronto-centric, Canada Blooms did strive to live up to its name by bringing in speakers from across the country, and this is how I got my muddy foot in the door, being put up at a nearby swank hotel and descending periodically to the convention centre in order to pontificate to audiences that sometimes numbered six hundred or more. Proceeds from the show went to support many civic gardening projects undertaken by the Garden Club of Toronto, which is an aspect of garden shows I especially appreciate.

Canada Blooms has evolved somewhat from the glory days of the nineties, as it's now combined with the National Home Show at a new location. But it still offers over two hundred hours of talks and demonstrations, though speakers now tend to be more local than previously (yes, I *do* miss my splish hotel). Nevertheless, it remains one of Toronto's top festival events and the tour buses continue to roll in.

But garden trends do come and go, and eventually the worm began to turn, as more and more enthusiasts came to realize just how much work and cost and commitment was involved in maintaining the splendid designer garden they'd installed. A great retraction ensued. Small specialty nurseries tumbled out of business. Gardening television shows dwindled. The glossy magazines either quit or morphed into patio décor advertisements. The bloom was off the rose. And while the really big shows, some after a period of wobbling, managed to survive the shift in mood, many succumbed to the inevitable. One of my favourite smaller shows to bite the dust was the annual "A Celebration of Island Gardening," put on by the Central Vancouver Island Botanical Gardening Society. Monies raised by this show went toward fulfilling the society's dream of creating a botanical garden in Nanaimo. Held in March in Nanaimo, the show had none of Toronto's expansive glitz, but did enjoy a wonderful neighbourliness and a hands-on practicality that had pruning-workshop participants gathered outdoors around a tree while an expert demonstrated. Besides workshops, there were commercial exhibits, educational programs and a speakers' series.

When it came to outdoor shows later in the season, coastal growers were for a while doubly blessed. The Victoria Flower and Garden Show, previously held indoors in downtown Victoria, moved outdoors to a couple of different locations, including a stint at Royal Roads University on the grounds of stately Hatley Castle, with the Strait of Juan de Fuca and snow-capped Olympic mountains as the perfect backdrop. Theme gardens, speakers and demonstrations, castle tours, a Japanese tea ceremony, a children's gardening zone and a market area on the lawn made for a delightful experience in a wonderful setting. But, unhappily, the show is no more.

Neither, alas, is Vancouver's VanDusen Flower and Garden Show, which in its heyday was the largest outdoor show in North America, covering eleven acres of the Great Lawn area of VanDusen Botanical Garden and drawing upward of twenty-five thousand people, with proceeds going to help support the garden. It too kicked off with a gala preview party, typically with a more West Coast bacchanalian flair than Toronto's tuxedo-and-gown affair. Among the show's many enticements were theme gardens, a marketplace, a master gardener's clinic, competitions, new plant introductions, an entertainment stage and horticultural, craft and speakers' pavilions. Food and cooking were featured as well, with many of the city's celebrity chefs holding forth in the Gourmet Gallery.

I miss these shows because they were wonderful gathering places for the gardening community. But times change, and I like how the issue of food security and sustainability has caught the imagination of a new generation of growers. Seedy Saturdays are booming, allotment and schoolyard gardens are thriving. Like many other communities, Denman's now blessed with an influx of smart new gardeners who are taking the growing of edibles to heights scarcely dreamed of back in the hazy seventies. Given the demands of the day, these are healthy developments, but I still miss my splish hotel room.

Wild Pursuits

NOTHING STIMULATES THE designing gardener's imagination more agreeably than an extended ramble through wild places. Nurseries, garden shows, tours and similar events all have their purposes, but none quite compares with the ancient wisdom to be gleaned from Mother Earth herself.

Long ago, garden master Lien-Tschen wrote: "The art of laying out gardens consists in an endeavour to combine cheerfulness of aspect, luxuriance of growth, shade, solitude and repose in such a manner that the senses may be deluded by an imitation of rural nature." Subscribing to a similar philosophy, Sandy and I took ourselves off for several weeks in March to absorb what we could of nature's late-winter beauty before the crush of our spring planting.

On Whidbey Island in Washington State's Puget Sound, we camped alone in a mature Douglas fir forest. Spaced widely apart, the stout old firs rose through a dense understorey of salal, the native broad-leafed shrub whose glossy green leaves are used in commercial floral arrangements. Growing in impenetrable thickets two metres tall, the salal formed softly undulating waves of green against which the emergent boles of the firs showed vividly. The kind of effect you could spend forever trying to achieve with clipping and shearing.

Walking along high sea cliffs in the same park, we frequently stopped to admire the gnarled limbs of firs dwarfed and twisted by wind. Increasingly, gardeners are recognizing the values of dead and dying "wildlife trees" as habitat for insects and the birds that feed on them, as well as for the various creatures that nest in their cavities. The gnarled sea-cliff firs, clinging to life in the teeth of wind and drought, reminded us that even in their extended death throes, old trees can be extraordinarily beautiful.

We hiked along headlands where grassy banks dropped a great depth to the sea, the smooth clarity of their descent as satisfying as a freshly mown lawn, contrasting with the sweep of water in a pleasing interplay of vivid green and shining blue surfaces. Sprawled on the grass of a high vantage point, we gazed down over an intensely farmed prairie defined by an unequivocal line where old-growth forest butted up against a meticulously tilled field. No feathering or buffering or gradual transitions here; rather the shaggy complexity of the forest cheek-by-jowl with the immaculate field, a stunning symmetry of opposites.

Barely surviving Friday-night rush-hour traffic through Seattle, we streaked southward toward Portland, then swung east through the Columbia Gorge, following the great river upstream into the high desert country of central Oregon. Here we entered a landscape of rolling sagebrush plains and immense lava buttes, almost as removed as we can get from the dripping rain forests of home. In this parched and windswept terrain, the landscape lessons were less by way of the startling contrasts we'd been captivated by on Whidbey, and more the subtle compatibilities deserts specialize in.

Junipers are widely admired for their hardiness and beauty—we have a few small specimens in the garden at home—and so we were delighted to find ourselves now camping in the largest old-growth juniper forest on the continent. Although many hundreds of years old, these juniper trees were generally less than ten metres tall, but exceptionally fine. Their densely packed blue-green needles showed stunningly against the silvery grey of sagebrush and bleached desert grasses.

Hiking along the base of a high lava butte, we came upon an enchanted wild garden of junipers growing amid enormous rocks that had tumbled from the butte and settled in patterns of casual perfection any rock gardener would drool to duplicate. At one spot, a huge rock was cleft entirely open, as though by the hand of a wrathful Jehovah, its twin sundered sections lying like an open book with a big juniper tree emergent between the two. You couldn't help but think of sacred places and events, precisely the kind of feeling the best of gardens excite.

Last year's juniper "berries" (they're actually fleshy female cones) created all sorts of pleasing effects. In places, they littered the ground under the trees, a vivid embroidery of plummy blue. We saw them scattered among tiny, yellow-blooming ephemerals, and in another spot mingled with small pink wildflowers whose name we didn't know. Both compositions were exquisite. So was the combination of berries still massed on junipers alongside rusty-orange catkins dangling from small alder trees growing on a riverbank. The berries and catkins together, with silvery sagebrush beneath, formed a simple yet splendid tableau.

The point for the gardener, of course, is not to try to duplicate these wild arrangements, but rather to absorb a sense of them, a feeling for how entirely correct they are in their place, and to have that sensibility inform our efforts as we move, however haltingly, toward gardening in harmony with natural landscape patterns.

For the Birds

ONLY A MISANTHROPIC misfit might propose that a garden would be better without birds; nevertheless, there lingers at least a ghost of ambivalence in even the most avian-aware gardeners. Because, notwithstanding the charm of their antics, their perfection of song and flight, the offbeat companionship they offer, birds can also be a damned nuisance in the garden.

I've complained for years, and shall continue to complain in the pages that follow, about the habits of American robins and towhees, their repeated ruining of our mulching schemes and pilfering of berries. Barred owls, whose nocturnal hootings haunt the springtime night, have a habit of perching in big trees around our clearing and repeatedly swooping into the yard to seize basking garter snakes. Thanks mostly to the owls, our snake population has plummeted, which is a disaster to any gardener who loves snakes for both their beauty and their prowess at devouring slugs.

But it's the woodpecker family that comes close to taking the blue ribbon for general mischief-making. Minor miscreants in the family include the flickers, who largely confine their incursions to devouring blue elderberries and courtship drumming on our satellite dish. Their big cousins, the pileated woodpeckers, are with us year-round and are especially welcome in winter, but less so in autumn when they set about chipping holes in the ripening apples, forcing us to harvest them prematurely.

No, the real hooligans in the woodpecker family are the red-breasted sapsuckers, a brightly plumed subspecies of the sapsuckers found all across the continent in breeding season. They make their living by drilling parallel rows of small holes into the bark sheathing the trunk or limbs of a living tree, later returning to drink sap pouring from the holes and eat any insects stuck to the sap. My bird book tells me they are "quiet, retiring and easily overlooked." That's scarcely the case at our place where every spring several pairs move in to court and nest nearby.

Noisy, brazen and destructive, they're about as easy to overlook as a mob of biker dudes in the kitchen.

They drill their holes in apple and crabapple trees, in cherries and plums, magnolias and even large lilac bushes. The holes take on a depressing aspect, like oozing pus, and can severely damage a tree by exposing it to fungal or other invasions. The bird's favourite food sources at our place are birch and mountain ash, whose thin bark they chip away in lozenge-shaped patches, leaving a scanty lattice-work between the holes. Over the years, they have killed two mountain ash outright by entirely perforating most of the trunks' bark, and have seriously crippled a couple of others. Our little copse of European white birches stubbornly clung to life despite repeated seasonal assaults by sapsuckers, but ended up so wizened and forlorn-looking that we eventually removed them for decency's sake.

Unlike most woodpeckers, sapsuckers seem not at all shy of humans. Tapping away at a trunk, they'll allow us to walk right up to them, almost close enough to touch them (and, believe me, I've been tempted). When startled, they utter a single, truncated cry like the wheeze of a scolding seagull and fly off with the pulsing flight pattern typical of woodpeckers.

Efforts at deterrence have proven futile. I've tried attaching fine mesh wire around the trunks of susceptible trees; I've repeatedly smeared the drill holes with tree-wound paste. But to no avail. The birds either drill fresh holes on unprotected parts of the trunk or switch to new trees. I've employed shouting, throwing stones—even, at one point, training a border collie to chase them off—without long-term success. I'm told there is a toxic substance that can be painted onto the trunk as a repellent. We haven't fallen to this foul resort (yet).

Neither have we descended to the tactic favoured by tyrants for millennia: destroying the homes of the enemy. We've always made a point of leaving certain large dead trees standing in the forest as "wildlife trees." Various woodpeckers excavate holes in the trees, in search of food as well as for nesting sites. These eventually accommodate other cavity nesters, both birds and mammals. But, resorting to the vernacular, it's a bit of a piss off that two of the most regular cavity tenants are among our worst tormentors: sapsuckers and denning raccoons. Despite provocations, we've spared the snags, but considerable rectitude has been required.

In a creative moment it occurred to me that a possible stratagem for outwitting the sapsuckers could arise from the notion of the sacrifice plant. This is a plant that one retains for the purpose of attracting pests to it in order that they'll leave more desirable plants alone. We've experimented with this in the veggie patch, using 'Red Russian' kale as sacrifice plants for aphids. Would a similar approach work with sapsuckers? Installing more mountain ash seemed the order of the day. Speaking frankly, in the sometimes brutal world of gardening *realpolitik,* I'd rather sacrifice a surplus mountain ash or two if by doing so we can save the magnolias, cherries and apples. Admittedly, this element of sacrifice-plant theory smacks of an end-justifies-the-means approach whose ethical implications it's probably wiser not to explore.

But here's the rub: Does one, by planting a species particularly attractive to certain pests, sometimes defeat one's purposes by encouraging additional pests? Will planting several more mountain ash, as we were now proposing to do, even knowing them to be doomed, keep the sapsuckers happy and allow our other trees to grow in peace? Or, will an expansion of their favourite food source simply encourage more sapsuckers to take up residence, their escalating populations eventually dooming other trees besides the mountain ashes? Is this the moral equivalent of dim-witted leaders making war in the name of peace?

If, on the other hand, one were to eliminate mountain ash as well as birch trees from the place—something the sapsuckers are well on their way to accomplishing already—would the wretched birds go elsewhere to find their favourite foods, or would they continue nesting close by and switch to attacking other prized trees? Experimentation in these areas is far more easily conducted with annuals and biennials than it is with trees, where a poor choice today could spell humiliation eight or ten years from now.

As I write, there's a sapsucker tapping away at the trunk of a gleditsia just in front of the house. I shan't run out and shout at it, or throw pebbles. I like to believe that I'm perhaps developing a more Zen approach to the matter. Or, in more realistic moments, I simply recognize that the sapsuckers have both outwitted and outlasted me.

Feat of Clay

I RECENTLY HAD a chance encounter with a young woman whose garden was encumbered with heavy clay soil. Daunted but far from defeated, she maintained an admirable stiff upper lip, as clay-based gardeners do, if they're not to despair. I've long maintained that dealing with heavy clay soil builds character and that every gardener might be a finer person for having a patch of rough clay to contend with.

Needless to say, our place has one, a low-lying area at the north end of the garden where our standard sandy gravel gives way to lumpish and intractable clay. I imagine it was once a prehistoric pool in which tree ferns flourished and brachiosauruses wallowed. A couple of big rambling roses have thrived there for years, but otherwise the area's been a bit of a disgrace, much of it given over to invasive lemon balm, hairy apple mint and variegated creeping dead nettle.

Heavy clay is almost always difficult to deal with. When wet it coheres like malignant gumbo; when dry it hardens to obstinate concrete. One looks for windows of opportunity for improving things, and indeed such a window opened for me when an uncharacteristic dry spell dehydrated the soil enough that it could be worked without compacting it badly. I first dug out the invasive ground covers—and received a welcome reprieve from what I had anticipated would be a protracted campaign. Revelling in surface moisture, the mint, dead nettle and lemon balm had each spread a thick matting of rootlets near the surface, but none had plunged deep into the clay. Using a heavy mattock I was able to rogue their roots out with relative ease.

Although a bully-boy attitude helps when tackling clay, care was required at this stage, as a number of creatures had settled in for the cold weather—a small greenish-brown tree frog hopped off unhappily over the disturbed earth, and between two sandstone blocks edging a bed I discovered a rough-skinned newt, torpid from the cold, its distinctive underside a gleaming yellow orange. These were

41

good omens, as were the abundant pink earthworms wriggling in the surface soil.

I spaded the whole bed over, plunging the spade blade deep, then turning up great podgy clods of clay. This is what old-timers would call "four-horse land"—ground so tough it would require four horses to break it in spring plowing. Particle size is the villain here. Clay particles are minuscule—a mere 0.002 millimetres or less, as compared to sand, which has particles ranging from 0.25 millimetres up to 1 millimetre. The finest garden loams contain approximately 50 percent sand mixed with some silt and clay, so the diversity of particle sizes creates abundant pore spaces in which air, moisture and organic bits can be held.

Once wet, clay can retain moisture for a very long time—and once dry can remain impervious to moisture for just as long. Its moist co-hesiveness is what makes clay perfect for nursery folk to use for balled and burlapped trees—the so-called B&B trees. I remember acquiring one such specimen years ago and heeding the expert advice of the day to simply plop the whole root ball into the ground. The tree lived all right, but for years grew at an unimaginably slow pace. Where it should have been seven metres high, it was still only two. Eventually I dug it out and, amazingly, most of the roots were still locked inside the clay ball. Only one adventuresome root had managed to break free and grow, and was probably the sole reason the tree was still alive. The problem here is that the extreme difference in soil texture between clay and the surrounding earth impedes water movement and inhibits root growth. Nowadays, whenever we acquire a B&B tree or shrub, I first bare-root it, systematically dissolving the imprisoning clay ball with a jet of water from a hose, before transplanting.

But back to our clay patch—which I suppose in hindsight we might have simply planted with compatible B&B trees and called it quits. The only alternative was to try expanding pore space by adding amendments. Organic matter being a cheap and effective soil conditioner for heavy clay, I first spread a thick layer of wood chips—about fifteen centimetres deep—over the whole surface. Some weeks earlier, we'd had a dump truck deliver eighteen cubic metres of shredded Douglas fir bark and sapwood from a pole yard on Vancouver Island. Ideally, you'd leave the stuff to decompose for a few years, but here I simply spaded it in, digging the bed over a second time, working it even deeper than the first dig. As attractive as it is to beneficial fungi and bacteria, decomposing wood waste sucks nitrogen out of the soil, so I next spread a layer of canola meal, followed by a thorough drenching of urine to boost available nitrogen.

Then began a veritable layer cake of amendments. Dolomite to sweeten the acid soil, as well as render it more porous and friable. A sprinkling of granulated bone meal for phosphorus (we've switched to rock phosphate in the meantime). A pinch of boron. Then some sand, though not as much as I would have liked. Ash and cinders are, along with sand, traditional amendments for breaking up clay soils, as well as a good source of potash and trace minerals, so I next spread a layer of wood ash saved from last winter's wood-stove burning. Then some precious leaf mould from the bigleaf maples. Finally I turned the whole works in by spading the bed for a third time. Already, by this digging, the soil had loosened and lightened tremendously. I planned to add compost and more wood ash in a few months' time.

For the moment, fortified with sufficient character building to get me through any other garden challenges the year might throw our way, I left the bed to the elements, for bacteria and fungi to set about breaking down the organic matter, opening up pore spaces and creating the crumbly, altogether gratifying state of good tilth.

Mushroom Magic

EVERY YEAR IT seems there are more and more mushrooms popping up at our place—spring morels in the vegetable patch, oyster mushrooms on old alder logs, fairy rings circling in the lawns and various unidentified fungi in undisturbed corners. I used to believe that having mushrooms in the garden was, like cockroaches in the house, a shameful thing, revealing one's lack of cleanliness and moral rectitude. But I've come full circle (the correct direction to come when dealing with fungi) and now rejoice to see mushrooms of all types fruiting wherever they will.

We've long appreciated the role of fungi as decomposer organisms in the woodlands that surround our yard—the tactical brilliance with which a succession of different fungi consume rotting logs and other forest debris, helping turn the corpse of an ancient tree into the soil from which a new generation of trees will spring. Then, a couple of decades ago, progressive foresters in the Pacific Northwest began publicly discussing how crucial some fungi are to healthy forests because of what is called their mycorrhizal characteristics, indicating a symbiotic association between trees and fungi. This is a mutually beneficial (or sometimes mildly pathogenic) relationship in which the tree's rootlets become sheathed in fungal hyphae that take on the role of root hairs, extending and vastly increasing the tree's ability to absorb nutrients from the soil. The fungus shares with the tree the foods it produces through enzyme digestion of organic matter, and in turn the tree shares with the fungus the foods it produces through photosynthesis. Forests with extensive mycorrhizal networks have been shown to be far healthier and more productive than areas where heavy-impact forestry has destroyed the magic fungal network underground.

Specialty gardeners have traditionally known that other plants enjoy similar associations with specific fungi, the degree of intimacy varying with different classes of plants. Orchids, for example, simply cannot be raised without the right fungus active in their soil (the mycorrhizal fungus must penetrate the cells of the orchid seeds before they can germinate). So the question naturally arises: Would more, perhaps even most, of our garden plants benefit from having mycorrhizal fungi around their roots? And, if so, what changes in gardening technique would we have to implement?

For an unequivocal opinion on these questions, we need look no farther than Washington state, where mycologist Paul Stamets has evolved into something of a mycelial shaman, promoting the benefits of fungi for everything from personal health to toxic-waste remediation. An intriguing combination of scientist, prophet and entrepreneur, Stamets passionately advances the rationale of gardening in cooperation with fungal allies. He believes some 90 percent of plants benefit from reciprocal relationships with fungi, a relationship that protects the plant from disease and enhances its ability to absorb water and nutrients. By clearing and constantly ploughing up land, he maintains, we destroy these vital fungi, thereby short-circuiting the plant's natural growth mechanisms and requiring that we promote plant growth through fertilizers and other artificial means. Reintroducing mycorrhizal fungi to the soil, he says, will promote faster growth, speed transplant recovery and reduce the need for fertilizers and other additives. Several companies, including Stamets's mail-order operation, Fungi Perfect, now market a number of specialized mycorrhizal-fungus products for the home gardener, ranging from mixtures for use in potting soil to products used directly on seeds.

If visionary mycologists like Stamets are correct in their assertions—and my forest-sharpened instincts incline me to believe that they are—the implications for our gardening are enormous. The first activity we'd want to curtail is this endless digging and rototilling of soil which, no matter how soul-soothing, plays havoc with any mycelial threads in the ground—not to mention greatly inconveniencing earthworms, beneficial predators like ground beetles and centipedes and innumerable microorganisms. Personally, I have a deep metaphysical attachment to the rituals of spading (something I'll expound upon later in this volume) so going cold turkey is a drastic measure I'm disinclined to entertain, at least for the moment, but I see it advancing upon me.

We'd move instead toward a no-till system, constantly applying to the surface fresh organic matter that cooperative fungi and other organisms would transform into soluble food for our plants. Who knows, we might also incorporate edible mushrooms into our plantings—maybe the garden oyster mushroom, *Hypsizygus ulmarius,* which can unlock nutrients from straw, sawdust and organic debris, feeding the roots of underlying plants and producing gourmet mushrooms at the same time. Talk about a win-win.

So, yes, notwithstanding all the gloom prevalent in this imperfect world, it's possible to imagine bright days ahead, lazy days when we may set aside our spades, relax our aching bods and dance together merrily among the fairy rings of magical mushrooms.

Those Who Live in Glass Houses

FOR YEARS WE'D realized that many's the day in our broody coastal climate when by far the nicest place to be is inside the greenhouse. You don't really fancy being cooped up indoors when the thrilling fingers of spring are running through the earth and animating the twigs of every tree and shrub. But a chill wind or damp clamminess may make the outdoors desirable only for vigorous activity. No, it's in the greenhouse, where the temperature's up and so are the seedlings, that the gardener is most satisfactorily ensconced in spring, as in fall too, or on any inclement day in between.

For the longest time we had a modest little greenhouse at our place, about three by almost four metres, attached to the house. Fashioned from stout 4×4 red cedar pieces supporting large sheets of tempered glass, like everything else around here it was constructed under the watchful eye of Parsimony. The structural members were milled from cedar logs on the property and the water-stained glass sheets cost five bucks apiece. The floor was composed of thick chunks of concrete-and-aggregate paving that used to be a neighbour's front path and made a dandy heat sink in the glass house. Total cost: about two hundred dollars—less than what we subsequently paid for a made in-China flimsy tubular metal and plastic greenhouse that we move around the veggie patch.

That old greenhouse had served us faithfully for three decades, but its time was done. After thirty winters of exposure to moisture, the cedar sills were rotting badly and the glass panes tending to rattle ominously in the wind. As well, certain design flaws were no longer tolerable. For instance, in our budget-driven construction phase, I had decided to "make do" with a primitive ventilation system on the roof, fashioned from a pair of old wooden frame windows that could be raised or lowered from inside via an attached pole. As with democracy, the price for this system was constant vigilance. Any rapid change in temperature in either direction involved being on hand to open or close the vents.

Finally tiring of this constant flirtation with disaster, I actually went so far as to purchase one of those automatic ventilator control thinga-mabobs about fifteen years ago, but never quite got around to installing it. The inadequate roof vents required leaving doors and windows open during extremely hot weather. Notwithstanding preventative measures, hummingbirds, butterflies, dragonflies, robins and other fauna insisted upon entering the greenhouse and then fluttering hopelessly against the south-facing glass in which there were no openings for escape. The on-going catch-and-release program necessitated by these intruders went hand in hand with the regimes of manual vent opening and closing, the two gobbling up absurd amounts of my time.

But, most pressingly, the glass house was always a tad too small for our purposes, a fact that my old dad had pointed out shortly after we'd constructed it. "Needs to be twice that size," he'd said, without being asked. (What's particularly aggravating about unsolicited advice from old dads is that it so frequently turns out to be correct.) In fact, the greenhouse, for all its shortcomings, was more or less adequate for horti-cultural purposes—germinating seeds, growing tomatoes and basil, and overwintering half-hardy ornamentals. What it lacked—and this would never have occurred to my old-school workaholic dad—was sufficient room for a pair of comfortable chairs, a reading light and perhaps a little bistro-style table at which one could take tea while keeping an eye on the garden.

Thus, one bright autumn day—when I was mere months beyond major surgery and should by rights have been lolling in delicious in-dolence—we set about knocking down the old greenhouse in order to re-place it with one twice as large. Not finding anything in the marketplace that fit our needs and budget, we decided to once again build our own, with construction help from an accomplished carpenter and friend. I won't belabour the chores involved—sledgehammering the old concrete apart, designing a building to suit our purposes, crawling around saw-mill yards for lumber and demolition yards for patio doors, figuring out where waterlines and electrical lines should run, and all the rest.

For walls, we reused all the tempered glass sheets from the old house, along with three sets of single-pane patio doors, leaving enough cash on hand to afford twin-layer polycarbonate roofing, which both moderates the interior temperature and does away with the condensation drips of glass roofing.

In for a penny, in for a pound, we elected to also tear out the adjacent sunken Mediterranean garden, fill the space with twenty-five cubic yards of pit run, every cubic inch of which had to be barrowed in, and lay pavers across the whole expanse. The rationale for this retrofit involved advancing age and the requirement to begin eliminating unnecessary steps and providing flatter, safer surfaces than the sandstone pavers and steps had done. Gardeners generally, and compulsive makeover people particularly, have a remarkable facility for justifying why a perfectly settled piece of landscape needs to be torn apart and put back together differently.

Anyway, out came some lovely old lavender and sage plants; out came two beautifully globular variegated boxwoods, planted long ago. Out came small carpets of creeping thymes. Most impressively of all, out came the several dozen sandstone pieces that we'd hauled in by hand thirty years ago and now were hauling back out again, amazed at how much weight the stones, like certain acquaintances, had put on during the interim. Partway through the greenhouse project, it occurred to us that the view from the solarium-in-the-making would be immeasurably enhanced if we were to construct a stone round tower connected to the terraced walls on the hillside opposite. Thus all the sandstone pieces extracted from the former Mediterranean garden were hauled over by wheelbarrow and reformatted into a stumpy round tower, vaguely but satisfyingly evocative of the redoubtable round towers of Ireland.

Ah, but this is a story of great labours that concludes most happily. Half the new glass house now serves the gardens, with a germination chamber for early seedlings and growing trays of mesclun mix in very early spring. Tomatoes, bell peppers, aubergines and basil fill the whole space during the summer. Parsley and kale for salads grow through winter alongside tender ornamentals brought indoors during the coldest weather. The automatic vent opener, finally put to use, along with an exhaust fan on thermostat control, makes the old days of manual vent operation a quaintly anachronistic memory.

True to our original vision, the other half serves as a solarium, with comfortable seating for leisurely reading on a Sunday afternoon and a far-infrared sauna to provide a cocoon of warmth and fine music after grisly winter workdays outdoors. The bed was an afterthought. We'd imagined it might perhaps serve for spring and autumn sleep, but a few nights in that charmed space quickly expanded the vision, and in fact we're now out there on all but the vilest winter nights. It's a splendid place for sleeping, with the gardens spread out before us, perchance moonlight spilling across them. As though one were slumbering beneath the trees, dreaming in greenery, awakening among grasses and flowers. It's become a place of unaccustomed comfort and idleness right within the garden itself, and, goodness knows, chore-laden gardeners deserve a bit of both.

CONTRAPTUAL NEGOTIATIONS

Farewell, Ancient Shredder

THE GENUINE SATISFACTIONS of gardening essentially derive from ensuring that moments of delight, and of occasional rapture, outnumber instances of loss and grief. As my earlier kvetching about sapsuckers attempted to illustrate, there is no shortage of misfortune in a garden. This past spring a favourite lilac shrub—whose scented blossoms had graced our yard for almost twenty years—suddenly lost heart and died just as she was about to bloom again. Accustomed to the arbitrariness of life and death, the gardener accepts such setbacks for what they are and, in the words of disgraced public figures, strives to "go forward."

But certain reversals cast a wider and more complicated pall. Such seemed to be the case for me when our golden age of shredding crashed to an abrupt and unexpected close. For the previous fifteen years or so, I'd enjoyed a charmed run of being able to dice up bulky garden debris —brittle fireweed and Jerusalem artichoke stalks, prickly raspberry canes, the floppy stems of foxgloves, delphiniums, summer phlox and all the rest—in a shredder. We had acquired this marvellous machine, after lengthy negotiations, from an inventive old gentleman in Victoria who had fashioned it in his backyard from steel plate. Painted fire-engine red and powered by a gasoline motor, it was armed with a heavy steel cutting blade that could voraciously slice and dice whatever twigs and small branches I stuffed into its maw.

When it was time to make compost, sheathed in protective gear, I'd drag the machine to where all the garden debris was stacked, fiddle with various knobs and levers, and then yank on a cord to fire the beast up. Its roaring and shaking was tremendous, its appetite for chewing bunched stalks to pieces so insatiable I called it Beelzebub, after the prince of demons and of dung. When our place was open on the island's annual home and garden tour, I lugged it out to be admired by the guys who'd come along with their wives despite having little interest in gardening.

Our compost heaps, composed of alternating layers of the shredder's green gold, along with kitchen scraps and output from our composting privy, were creations of incontestable excellence. Within days of construction, they'd be steaming with heat, and would eventually convert their contents into rich, dark, crumbly compost. At the very heart of that great transformation, and thus at the heart of the garden itself, squatted the shredder.

But, unhappily, and it seemed tragically, this epoch of excellence came to an abrupt end. I was out in the yard shredding dutifully on a bright spring afternoon when suddenly there came a sharp clattering and god-awful banging inside the chamber. I shut the machine down and investigated, dismayed to discover that half the great whirling blade had sheared off completely. I dragged the mutilated shredder to a machine shop but was told that repair was impossible because of the way the chamber had been welded together originally. In one fell stroke, like Lucifer banished from heaven, I'd fallen from paradise. In anybody other than a gardener, post-traumatic stress disorder might have been an inevitable reaction to this stunning turn of events.

Ah, yes, the uninformed observer might remark, but surely you can acquire another shredder and carry on as before? Alas, no. For my disabled shredder had been one of a kind, a unique contrivance of muscular brute force whose like will not be seen again. Part of its efficiency derived from a complete disregard for safety issues—a moment's inattention might easily have cost me a few fingertips or even a whole hand—whereas commercial models seem designed primarily to prevent anyone from losing a fingernail and then suing the manufacturer for millions. I've examined some of the shredders for sale at respectable retail outlets, but they have excited only dismay and contempt. To replace our masterpiece with one of those abysmally flimsy knock-offs would be to concede that the universe is unfolding in ways that you would rather it not.

An added consideration, admittedly, is that the old shredder was a carboniferous monster, gulping oil and gasoline and spewing out polluting fumes like our own private tar sands. The biosphere is a better place without it. I like to imagine that in the days to come some inventive genius will design a solar-powered shredder or, in a perfectly closed loop, a shredder powered by the methane gas emitted from the compost heap.

In the interim, we've parked the decommissioned shredder in an out-of-the-way corner as a monument of sorts. Meanwhile, I'm reduced to a more hands-on and time-sensitive approach to compost making. For a while, I tried chopping leggy plant material by hand, employing an axe blade that's welded onto the end of a steel pipe and driven down vertically, as though one were pounding maize. But the work was arduous and primitive and roiled my heart with unseemly longing for the old days of shredding. Determined not to complain, nor to brood unduly over all that's been lost, instead we worked out a system in which woody material like raspberry canes or fireweed stems no longer go into the compost heap, but rather are consigned to a solitary spot where they're free to take as long as they require to rot down. Everything else—leafy greens, kitchen scraps, the compost-privy products—goes into the compost heap as before, but in a far quieter and more dignified fashion. Truth to tell, I don't really miss the roaring of Beelzebub, nor its noxious fumes, nor the sense of frenzy its clamouring induced. Once again, the making of compost is a more poetic, less mechanized affair. I see this as one small personal step away from fossil-fuel dependence and toward a cleaner and quieter environment, a transformation of loss and grief, if you will, into new and improved possibilities.

Barrowing Along

SOMETIMES IT FEELS as though the gardener's principal occupation is the picking up of materials, often heavy or bulky, and transporting them across uneven ground in order to deposit them someplace else. In this work, few tools prove more dutiful than the wheelbarrow. Known as far back as ancient Greece and China, for thousands of years the wheelbarrow has done its work with primitive but marvellous simplicity. More essential than sexy, it trundles faithfully behind the scenes while other fads and fashions flutter for the cameras.

Around our workplace, we're a two-wheelbarrow family. One unit is built like a Sherman tank, with rugged steel frame and heavy-gauge steel bucket. During the thirty-plus years we've had it, this brute has moved more weight than the builders of Stonehenge. Its old bucket is now perforated with rust holes, but it barrows on and I dread the day when it can go no farther. The other is a younger and flimsier affair with a smaller wheel, wooden frame and a lighter-gauge steel bucket. It's what passes for a wheelbarrow nowadays and dozens of its type line the entranceways of big-box stores in spring. Some have a polypropylene bucket. Some have two wheels. None impress. For sturdiness is of the essence, and a good wheelbarrow—like our old trustworthy—should last for decades, if not generations. The built-in obsolescence of the flimsy barrows now on offer is an insult to the great legacy of barrowing and contemptible to any true-blue barrow-man or -woman.

One of my main barrow tasks is wheeling in the winter firewood. No road penetrates our woodlot and the big barrow is perfect for navigating narrow footpaths and rolling over tree roots (something at which low-slung and long-snouted ersatz barrows are hopeless). It's work enough getting in the hundred-plus loads required to fill the woodshed every autumn, without the added aggravation of periodically ramming into a protruding rock or root.

Moving massive stones from place to place often requires innovative measures. If a stone's too heavy to be picked up and placed in the barrow, I use a roll-and-jerk technique, much like an Olympic weightlifter. The barrow is laid on its side and the stone rolled onto the edge of the bucket. Then bucket and stone are jerked upright together. If a hernia isn't induced by the lifting, it may be by subsequent wobbling around with the overloaded barrow. Tipping techniques can be tricky too. Unless meticulously tipped, a load of precious compost or fresh cement may disgorge sideways, entirely missing the intended point of deposition.

The Old English noun "barrow" also means a hill or hillock, but wheelbarrows and hills don't go well together. Pushing a loaded barrow uphill can bring a dismaying sense of gradual momentum loss, followed by teetering uncertainty as inertia's about to defeat you, then a grunting stall. Getting a running head start at an impending incline sometimes helps. Descending a hill, the opposite's true, as gravity tries to wrench the barrow from your grip and send it careening downhill. Disaster can sometimes be averted by pressing the barrow legs into the earth to try to brake the runaway barrow. On wet or icy ground the downhill slide may be a thing of terrifying beauty.

Mastering the intricacies of barrow operation can take longer than getting a medical diploma. Novices may be observed repeatedly picking up items and carrying them over to a barrow, rather than wheeling the barrow to where the items are. Some people take years to figure out it's easier to point a barrow in its intended direction before loading it up. They'll load to the brim and then get a herniated disc trying to turn the barrow around. Or they'll load up in a spot so tight it can't be turned around at all. Dragging a barrow backwards indicates an education considerably short of complete. Strategic reversing, on the other hand, is indicative of a sophisticated wheeler. When our woodshed's almost full, I take satisfaction in first wheeling around and then reversing into the shed's narrow passage so that pieces can be conveniently unloaded without a knee-knocking barrow intervening.

In the end, disposition of an old wheelbarrow requires careful consideration. Our first barrow was an ancient contraption with a steel wheel but no tire and a flat wooden bed into which wooden sides could be slotted. When we replaced it long ago, we burned it—only to later discover in a posh gardening magazine a photograph of an identical model gaily painted and planted with nasturtiums and available for a small fortune. So when in due course another old barrow came our way, we gussied it up with fresh paint, filled its bucket with *objets trouvés* and made it an installation in the flower garden. This is what passes for the wisdom of age.

But one could do far worse than spend one's allotted time as a barrow-person. The fresh air. The exercise. The mental equilibrium. Having a wheelbarrow is almost like having a personal trainer. Then, after a long life of barrowing, it would be fitting to spend your declining days like one of those wizened oldsters pictured in "developing" countries, being wheeled around the marketplace while reclining in a wheelbarrow. That would be the wheel deal.

Cutting Loose

THE CUTTING AND lopping of superfluous branches or twigs from vines, trees and shrubs, to promote flowering and fruitfulness or to induce a particular shape, may be a dominant part of the gardener's early spring. Because smooth pruning demands deployment of the right tool for each job, an avid pruner's tool kit typically contains an impressive arsenal of cutting devices. On our grounds, finicky snipping is accomplished with ikebana scissors whose slender blades can poke into scarcely penetrable places. We keep half-a-dozen pairs on hand, as they're useful for any number of ancillary jobs, from cutting twine to shamelessly slicing destructive black slugs in half.

But these lightweights have their limits, and heavier cutting requires pruning shears or secateurs, which is where trouble begins. Most secateurs are, like computer viruses, designed by sociopaths. I keep as evidence a pair of old anvil pruners whose blade chops down against a flat surface. Rather than a clean cut, these brutes invariably give any twig they encounter a tip of mashed pulp. They're intended for removing deadwood, where a clean cut is unnecessary, or for doing preliminary clips thus saving wear and tear on your superior secateurs, but I find them extremely annoying, particularly as they're often the only pruners you can lay your hand on when a clean cut's called for.

Where precise slicing is required, bypass blades are a better bet. Here one is required to choose between a well-crafted and expensive pair or the el-cheapo variety forever on sale as loss leaders in unimaginative gardening outlets. With parsimony our guiding star, we have traditionally gravitated toward the less-expensive alternative, which prove perfectly serviceable for the first half-dozen cuts. But the blades, fashioned near outer Shanghai from recycled mufflers and tailpipes, soon lose their edge. Each cut becomes a clasp wherein the target twig, rather than being severed cleanly, is pinched between the blades and refuses to let go.

A further annoyance is how the spring, inadequately implanted between the handles, periodically leaps free and lands at a distance from which it can be recovered, if at all, only after an extensive ground search.

Finally fed up with wayward springs and clasping cuts, one year I threw economic caution to the winds, purchasing a pair of designer secateurs with cherrywood handles and glittering steel blades that might have been forged at the anvil of Vulcan himself. Thus equipped, I became capable of astonishing keenness of cut. I felt I was, in Thomas Carlyle's words, wielding "the scissors of Destiny."

Alas, 'twas not to last. Unlike the garish orange plastic handles of its forerunners, this tony pair's hardwood handles had an uncanny knack for camouflage. They were impossible to spot when left unattended in the garden, requiring lengthy searches whenever mislaid. After a brief career with us, they disappeared completely. Eventually I discovered their charred remains amid the ashes of the rose prunings. From fire they'd come and to fire returned. My lesson learned, I shuffled back to the familiar torments of the el-cheapos.

Loppers are required for branches too thick to be cut by secateurs. For years I employed an ancient pair of wooden-handled loppers inherited from my dad. When they finally succumbed to the frailties of age, I bought a pair of techno-loppers large enough to fell a giant sequoia. Their chief drawback is they're impossible to get into tight corners, because the handles open so wide, and it's remarkable how many stout stems and branches are too tucked away to be vulnerable to long-legged loppers. Visiting the in-laws on one occasion, I did some pruning for them with their newfangled pair of ratcheting loppers, both agile enough to reach into awkward spots and powerful enough to sever sizable branches. I would have been tempted to acquire a pair, had I not already learned my lesson with the high-toned secateurs.

Since our garden is an arboraceous affair, we're constantly required to prune out tree branches high in the air. For decades I used an antique hardwood pole pruner with a tiny hooked blade controlled by a heavy-gauge wire running down the shaft. Eventually requiring something both longer and lighter, I bought a telescoping pruner that can reach almost four metres high. Both the complex lever system atop the pole and the thin rope that controls the blade have a dreadful tendency to get entangled in every branch they approach. Many's the time I'm left yanking murderously on the pruner, trying to extricate it from the tree, while hurling vile curses into the canopy.

The pole pruner came with a curved pruning saw that you're supposed to be able to attach to the top of the pole for sawing off branches too thick for the pruner. No coherent instructions were included and, despite my best efforts, the saw blade, like certain stubborn bachelors, refused to become attached. Eventually I affixed the blade to a long cedar pole instead and can now quite serviceably reach three or more metres up in order to saw off unwanted branches. For thicker limbs I bring out my chainsaw and orchard ladder and ascend amid the roaring to stare in the face of death by misadventure.

For all of these cutting devices, it goes without saying, sharpness of blade is of the essence. I'd profoundly appreciate having an itinerant scissors-grinder visit the neighbourhood periodically, as I remember one doing in my boyhood in England. No such luck. An occasional swipe at the blade with a rusty file must suffice and off I charge, wielding my delinquent pole pruner like a jousting knight his lance, along with our various dull scissors of Destiny.

All Strung Out

IF YOU HAPPEN to be sitting around in conversation with a cluster of theoretical physicists, chances are the talk will eventually turn to string theory, a construct in which strings replace the notion of elementary particles in quantum field theory. It's really rather charming to see how uncharacteristically lyrical physicists can become when discussing the supersymmetry of string functions and string cosmology.

Such talk might seem hugely abstruse to the uninitiated, but to the average gardener the string theory of physicists is a preoccupation of simpletons when compared to the twisted realities of garden string work. Few components are more crucial to ultimate success in a garden than the adept deployment of string, but opportunities for miscalculation lurk in every strand and filament. There's many a gardener who gets hopelessly strung out on the matter of string.

Consider type of twine for starters. Ideally, one wants a sturdy, organic, unobtrusive and long-lasting class of cordage adaptable to the multiple tasks at hand. A twine tensile enough to support a row of bullish broad beans but sufficiently subtle to disappear among the tendrils of clematis. Such a twine is unknown to humankind at this point in our evolution.

In its place we are cursed with various inferior lines of twine, notably the ubiquitous "garden twine" dyed a sickly seaweed green and retailed in prim little spools for a princely sum. Within weeks of being unstrung outdoors, the twine's green colouring has leached out, leaving an unsightly string the colour of a rodent's tail. Long before the growing season's over, the string enters a stage of premature degeneration in which the slightest touch may cause it to snap. One year, I sought to economize by purchasing an enormous spool of the dyed-green stuff. For a week or two, all went well as the string released smoothly from the hollow centre of the spool. But soon the centre could not hold and the whole spool collapsed in upon itself like a black hole from which it was impossible to extract any length of string before encountering a monstrous entanglement. The alternatives are an insufficient bunch of synthetic strings or heavy-handed hemp or jejune jutes.

Tormented as I had been by inferior twine, string cosmology eventually intervened on my behalf. Wandering the spectacular beaches of Pacific Rim Park one day, I found at my feet a long spool, or perhaps it was a bobbin, of twine, never used, and apparently designed for use on a machine. The twine was ample enough to serve all our stringy needs and durable enough to be reused for three years. Just as its usefulness was drawing to a close, we revisited the West Coast beaches and, yes, the thundering surf threw up another unused spool of similar twine. Those not conversant with string theory might mistake these events for coincidence, but I think not.

Even when the gods throw you a lifeline like this, or you find a superior quality of string at a reasonable price (late in the game, I did discover the merits of the black twine used by fisher folk to repair their nets), other problems soon arise. Issues of timing, for example. Is it too early to be tying the delphiniums? Few sights are more ridiculous than tiny shoots tentatively peeping from the ground and surrounded by a looming palisade of sticks and string. Or am I too late? Just when you're in the shed searching for some suitable string, the towering stalks of foxtail lilies, listing too long without support, abandon hope of reinforcement and topple to the earth. Have you employed too much string? As when a weakly herbaceous peony flower peeks forlornly through a network of supportive strings. Or too little? A hyperactive golden hops laughs maniacally at your tentative attempts at ties that bind it to its trellis.

If you string your string too high, a limpid clematis stretches like a trapeze artist for support, falls short, loses heart and dies back to the ground. Tied insufficiently high, the languid flowering stalks of *Stipa gigantea* trip over your low-slung lines and snap their slender stems. Failure to tie sufficiently tight can result in blue anchusas flopping and toppling from being given enough rope to hang themselves. Cinched too tightly to a stake, hog-tied 'Big Beef' tomatoes slowly strangle.

Nothing in string theory is more problematic than knotting. Ideally, one wants to employ a clever knot such as sailors use—a loop knot or reef knot or running knot—one that's speedily affixed and easily undone. Instead, you often as not end up with insufficient string to complete a proper knot, so the ends are barely connected and will soon let loose.

Or the great loop of twine you're attempting to affix around a sprawling shrub is stretched so tightly you need a third hand to tie the knot while the other two hold the tugging string ends. Or the comic effect created when one hand's holding up a wayward plant and the other is single-handedly attempting to undo an entanglement of string by flicking it like a bullwhip. Once tied, every knot does one of two things: either it unravels overnight, typically with disastrous consequences, or it refuses to be untied, when required, no matter how long you pick at it with broken fingernails.

Perhaps most problematic of all for the sustainable gardener is the compulsion to reuse string. Once the broad beans have been harvested, I gather up their several hundred metres of supporting twine by winding it around a stick. Then off I go to cinch and pinion various shrubs and trees, merrily oblivious to the fact that the time-tested twine will surely decompose before its intended secondary purpose is accomplished. Every pocket in my work clothes bulges with assorted scraps of old string so that in any emergency I always have some at hand, if only I can get it untangled. Most of these scraps will snap in short order, resulting in further emergency restringing with similarly derelict scraps. Oftentimes numerous scraps get knotted together to form a superscrap whose likelihood for failure is compounded exponentially by the vulnerability of each component piece.

Small instances of compensation do occasionally occur, as when I came upon a stringy installation in a celebrated Gertrude Jekyll garden in England. A tiny plant crouched beneath a circle of sticks amid a spiderweb of unsightly string, providing ample evidence that even in high places the snares of string await.

Nowhere amid these travails is there any evidence of the supersymmetry of string cosmology, such as I twice experienced on the beach. Quite the reverse, as highly strung gardeners become increasingly unstrung by the complexities of horticultural string theory.

War and Peace

GARDENERS, FOR THE most part, tend to be gentle folk, lovers of peace little drawn to the clash of arms or roar of conflict. Until provoked. And nothing provokes more rousingly than acts of vandalism in the garden. Discovering plants battered about by brazen intruders can stir instincts of murderous retaliation in even the most pacifist of plantspeople. Raccoons will do this to a person. They have done it to us recently and to dozens of our fellow islanders whose vision of the good life involves the raising of one's own fruits and vegetables.

For years, there was not a single raccoon on our little island. We gardened happily, vexed only on occasion by the normal travails of capricious weather, pestilential insects and periodic diseases. In hindsight I'm chastened by how largely indifferent we remained to the trials faced by gardeners elsewhere, the tribulations of *Procyon lotor*. In my very first book, I wrote with benign acceptance about raccoons, lacing my liberal views with affectionate descriptions, such as "their forepaws are the deft and delicate instruments of a tactile maestro."

Then the troubles began. By ways and means no one fully understands (or admits to), raccoons appeared near the south end of the island some years ago. Chicken houses were raided, plum trees stripped of ripe fruit. One resident claimed to have intercepted a raccoon hauling off a full-grown goose. Anecdotal evidence was amassed concerning declining songbird populations due to raccoons stealing eggs and killing birds. Shamefully, those of us not yet directly afflicted carried on blithely, as though the dark clouds of war massing on the horizon would somehow pass us by.

Then a stunning blow. Over the course of several nights, all our ripe grapes disappeared save for a few scattered on the ground. In denial, I imagined some hitherto unknown bird was to blame. Shortly after, two little pear trees in the vegetable patch had their lower limbs savagely broken off and stripped of fruit. I concluded this was the work of a genetically modified buck that had been successfully pole-vaulting into the veggie patch in the weeks previous (helpful conservation authorities having reportedly brought to the island a number of oversized bucks to "upgrade" our diminutive deer). But when an Italian prune plum tree was burglarized overnight of its ripening plums, the evidence was irrefutable: raccoons had sought us out at last. The rapid disappearance of goldfish from the pool and the telltale morning evidence of snails' shells scattered along the pool's edging confirmed the worst. Abandoning denial, we swung wildly over to obsessive paranoia, so that every mishap in the yard was attributed to coons. As happens in other contexts, the presumption of innocence was readily jettisoned in favour of uninformed revenge.

Nevertheless, most of the mischief can in truth be charged to coons. Gardeners might perhaps entertain some measure of forbearance if this nocturnal raider merely took what it needed and left the rest. But the coon's a vandal as well as a thief, smashing branches and spoiling more food than it can eat. It will wantonly massacre a whole flock of chickens, leaving most uneaten. It will pluck scores of fruits or tear off dozens of ears of sweet corn and take only a nibble from each before discarding it.

Two approaches are possible for the coon-confronted gardener. The defensive option calls for beefed-up fortifications. Lights can be left shining all night among vulnerable fruits. Stout wire cages may be erected around smaller targets. I've found that wrapping slick metal sleeves, such as old stovepipe, around the trunks of fruit trees can defeat these skilful climbers. Some growers swear by an electric fence as the only reliable deterrent. One helpful observer reported to me that he'd had good results spreading ground habanero pepper that would so irritate the coons' tender feet they'd avoid the area. But the raccoon displays dismaying persistence and ingenuity in pursuit of favourite foods, and the contraptions of deterrence, like a hapless missile defence shield, offer slender hope of permanent protection.

Hence the allure of the second option. The best defence is a good offence. Taking the fight to the enemy. Smoking him out. Slightly unbalanced by the losses we'd suffered, I began roaming our winter woods, fully prepared to fell any snag I suspected contained a raccoon den. Similarly besieged, some gardeners talk hard talk about bringing in fierce dogs to patrol the grounds at night. The very same horticulturist who used to be morally torn over having to dispatch a slug is now observed eyeing rifles and shotguns in the local hunting and fishing store. Traps are obtained, to be baited with fish or an egg or a piece of honey-soaked bread. Since catch and release is not a realistic option on a small island like ours, disquieting questions arise over what might be done with any trapped intruders. The good old boy down the road who's got antlers and animal heads hanging on every wall is suddenly the darling of the neighbourhood. A pacifist of the past, the hardened gardener now has an uncharacteristically tough glint in his eye, swaggering around gunslinger-style and challenging the raccoons to "bring it on."

But just as the posse is preparing to saddle up, the peace-loving naturalist side of the gardener restates the desirability of living in harmony with all creatures native to one's environment. Benign alternative techniques are reconsidered. Reflection occurs on the self-defeating nature of all violence. You overhear Buddhists whispering in the woods about the indwelling divine of all life. Like humankind at large, the besieged gardener hangs in the balance, torn between the instincts of war and peace.

Tooling Around

I'M FEELING UNCHARACTERISTICALLY pleased with myself just now, because last fall and for the first time ever, I managed to properly prepare our lawn mower for the coming year. After the final cutting in October, I hauled the machine to someone in town who knows the subtleties of gasoline-fired equipment. Ideally, one wouldn't possess such things...but for the near term they remain, unhappily, essential to maintenance of the homestead, so the least one can do is ensure they run as cleanly and efficiently as possible. My man expertly sharpened the blade, cleaned the air filter and carburetor, replaced the spark plug, flushed the oil and gas tank, and generally inspired in me a gratifying sense that I was doing right by the machine. Thus far it has been performing admirably, with none of the hysteria traditionally associated with trying to get a lawn mower to start immediately and run smoothly after a winter of neglect.

The proper care of garden tools and equipment is an art unto itself, founded on the critical trinity of cleaning, sharpening and storing. In ideal circumstances, these functions would be rigorously sustained throughout the gardening year, and especially in autumn—the perfect, if seldom practical, time for getting the tool shed in order. But for those of us pulled in too many directions by the contrary winds of fall, not to mention the mania of spring or the lassitude of summer or somnolence of winter, you do your best and to hell with the rest.

Thorough cleaning of tools is a *sine qua non*. Mud-caked spades, forks, trowels and the like should be washed in warm soapy water. Rust spots that may have developed ought to be thoroughly scrubbed with steel wool. Wiped dry with an old towel, the metal parts should be rubbed with an oil-soaked rag to inhibit further rusting. While you're at it, any wooden handles could use a bit of oiling as well, to discourage cracking. Don't mistake me: I seldom perform any of these niceties myself, but the advice is unassailable.

Sharpening is very much to the point too. None of us need to be told that a modest investment of time spent sharpening all cutting implements soon pays huge dividends when it comes to getting yardwork done quickly and efficiently. It's generally recommended that mower blades and shears be professionally honed; we amateurs can certainly sharpen other implements ourselves, and I'm not beyond taking a supplementary swipe at the mower blades and shears once they've become desperately dull. Sharpening is best tackled with a pair of thick gloves and a sturdy bench vise to hold potentially lethal weapons such as sickles and machetes. (Does anyone this side of Cuba actually use a sickle or machete anymore? I have two of each, but probably spend at least as much time sharpening them as swinging them.) Several files of different sizes are used for sharpening spades, hoes and hand pruners, while the cut above deploy a whetstone for putting an edge on other blades.

Intelligent tool organization likewise saves time and frustration in the long term. Spades, forks, rakes and the like are best hung flat against a wall. Smaller tools can be hung on pegboards. If you're short on wall space, a big old barrel or garbage can is useful for holding long-handled implements in a way that allows you to easily spot the one you're after. I try my best in this regard, but am repeatedly sabotaged by the reprehensible tendency to toss tools indifferently into the shed after a hard day's labour. Over the course of time, this methodology results in unmitigated chaos sharpened by repeated threats of divorce. But I'm really at an unfair disadvantage by virtue of having three small sheds and never quite remembering what tool is in which shed. Wandering among the three, I frequently disremember what tool I'm looking for, and certainly have little time left over for straightening things up.

But even without such hazards, the impulse to clean and organize tools, praiseworthy as it is in itself, can run us into other difficulties. Tidying the tool shed invariably brings on painful decisions about old treasures that no longer have practical value but are nonetheless still gratifying to have at hand. The machetes and sickles are at least one step above this, but ancient spade blades with broken handles are not. They remain in place because one foresees someday extricating the embedded handle stub and replacing it with a stout new handle, if only you could buy a new handle for substantially less than a new spade. Similarly, a rake that's only a few tines short will surely come in handy sometime down the road.

For years we kept two derelict lawn mowers in a shed, neither of which had the faintest hope of ever cutting grass again, but both of which held out great promise of being converted into leaf shredders or even antique lawn ornaments. Laugh if you want, but not long ago I spotted in an upmarket gardening magazine (perhaps the very one with the glam barrow) a photograph of an old rotary mower like ours installed on a lawn with petunias growing from the hopper into which grass clippings were thrown in better days. Unreliable stepladders splashed with paint came similarly into vogue as pot stands. As a consequence, one hangs onto archaic bow saws and hoes and all sorts of other rubbish in the expectation that they'll someday make fashionable garden art once the arbiters of taste have given them the nod. In this spirit, but not even waiting for approval by the arbiters, Sandy recently absconded with a trove of our (my) old tools, now more venerable than useful, painted all of them fire-engine red and hung them en masse on the outer wall of an old shed. Although I'd initially resisted the scheme as somehow un-seemly, the effect was quite agreeable, becoming a much-photographed attraction during a subsequent garden tour.

Short of such artistic audacity, a clean sweep is preferable to having the shed cluttered with useless implements, as is maintaining your func-tioning tools in a cleaned, oiled, sharpened and properly stored state. The same school of thought holds that if you buy high-quality tools in the first place and look after them diligently, they'll give far more years of service per dollar spent than you'd get with a succession of cheap al-ternatives, which one tends not to look after very well because they cost so little in the first place.

In this regard, I'm personally betwixt and between. Abhorrence to-ward the throwaway culture is still not quite sufficient to incline me toward spending top dollar for designer tools (I reference the debacle of our cherrywood-handled secateurs). Indeed, some of my most reli-able implements are ones inherited from my dad and now well over a half-century old. Not as meticulous in my care of tools as I might be, I have all the more reason to indulge in self-congratulation when, as is currently the case with our finely tuned lawn mower, I do on occasion do things the way they ought to be done all the time.

The Great Gate Debate

CERTAIN DECISIONS TO be taken in the garden are more daunting than others and few carry heavier baggage than the question of what garden gate to install. I'm particularly alert just now to the hazards involved because several of our decrepit old gates are close to becoming unhinged. Something plainly must be done about them. But just what?

Thirty years ago, I quickly roughed together the now-tottering gates by stretching stucco wire across a rough cedar frame. Their mission statement was simplicity itself: keep the damn deer out. Considered "good enough for now," the gates were slated to be replaced eventually by something sturdier, more permanent and artistic, more in keeping with the elevated tone of the garden as a whole. Now, more than a quarter century and any number of emergency repair jobs later, the day appears to be at hand.

But the options and the implications are formidable. One could decide on a traditional prim lattice gate with an arched top, or perhaps something more imposing worked in wrought iron and hung on brick pillars. A monastic-style solid-wood door beneath a gothic arch would certainly make a statement and a Chinese moon gate would be out of this world. Or maybe something hand-forged from scrap-metal parts, incorporating pieces of driftwood and stained glass. The list of possibilities is all but inexhaustible.

One fundamental problem is that whatever gate we install may now aspire to far grander ambitions than merely keeping the deer at bay. Certainly protection is at the heart of any gate's reason for being. High-tech entries with electronic sensors and security keypads are a modern version of keeping the barbarians outside the gates, but are hardly what's called for in a bucolic situation like ours.

Firstly, we gate creators must ask ourselves: Is the gate (and the fence or wall of which it is a part) intended to promote a sense of privacy and enclosure, or rather to be transparent and inviting to visitors and passersby? Beyond plain slothfulness, one of the reasons we've stuck so long with our flimsy stucco-wire variations is that they're marvellously see-through, allowing the surrounding landscape to flow seamlessly into the garden. In their place, solid wooden gates, no matter how elegant, would partially exclude this borrowed landscape.

Along with its blunt practical functions, a gate also makes a statement about the gardens and dwelling to which it gives entry. Frequently it is the first garden component a visitor encounters and from which a first impression is formed. Elaborate iron gates hinged on stone pillars bespeak power and privilege, while a handcrafted Asian bamboo gate gives promise of a garden of contemplative repose. A whimsical little rustic gate hints at entry into a secret garden full of innocent delights and wonders.

The guiding principle in this regard is obvious: let the gate fit the garden and let both be appropriate to the house. Magnificent gates opening upon a diminutive or unkempt garden immediately betray delusions of grandeur. A solemn moon gate disclosing a yard of garish annuals and tacky bric-a-brac renders the unfortunate gatekeeper a laughingstock.

I almost fell into this very trap myself not long ago as I was gazing admiringly at an array of gorgeous gates meticulously handcrafted from red cedar by a fellow islander. But, lovely as they were, in our rambling garden of weathered wood and moss-covered stones, these elegant gates would have hung in splendid incongruity.

To further muddy the gate debate, there are weighty metaphysical considerations in the matter of gates. It's no coincidence that various religious traditions speak of the gates of paradise through which the pure of heart alone may enter. And more than one insightful observer has proposed that by entering the garden, one is in a way entering into one's inner self.

Historically, poets have shown a persistent tendency to congregate around garden gates. Tennyson pleads: "Come into the garden, Maud, / I am here at the gate alone." American poet Ella Wheeler Wilcox reminisces: "Back on its golden hinges / The gate of Memory swings / And my heart goes into the garden / And walks with the olden things." Richard Crashaw wonders: "What heaven-entreated heart is this, / Stands trembling at the gate of bliss...?"

Personally, I'm trembling at the gate of indecision. With possibilities pouring in from all directions, like gatecrashers at a rowdy teen house party, I'm seriously thinking of doing yet another last-ditch repair job on our tottering relics and perhaps searching for enlightenment beyond the garden gate.

Divisions of Labour

AS THE GROWING season revs up into high gear, certain households may already be entangled in vexing questions about who is responsible for what in the garden. People who live, or at least garden, in solitude are spared these thorny considerations, but for the rest of us, the coming months stretch like a minefield of explosive possibilities.

The fundamental issue concerns authority: Who's in charge here? Certain people like to control everything, so it's no surprise that they'd include the garden in their empire, but why would anyone else want to play servant to their master? I mean, gardening itself can be vexing enough without having a tyrant prowling around assigning chores and criticizing one's best efforts.

Oh, but the companions of bossy gardeners can be terribly clever at ducking out of assignments. Faked plant allergies, for example, provide a very effective escape mechanism. So can a bad back. The need to visit ailing friends or relatives in distant places can also make a legitimate albeit temporary alibi, in a way that wanting to go play golf seldom does. Those too timid to risk insubordination may strike a compromise of sorts, agreeing to do only the most basic of tasks like digging holes or wheelbarrowing rubbish away. Headphones or earbuds playing music at extremely high volume are a useful accessory in these circumstances.

Some benign despots master the art of exercising absolute control over every aspect of garden design and maintenance without ever appearing to do so. These are generally females of considerable expertise and great cunning. They know precisely how a garden ought to appear and function, but are far too nimble to just say so. Instead, they consult with whoever else is involved, they brainstorm, they work toward consensus decision-making, and if in the final analysis the decision is made to plant the PeeGee hydrangea in this precise spot and no other, anyone else involved comes away feeling wonderfully empowered over having participated in a decision that had already been made long before their opinion was sought.

One time-honoured division of labour in households of more than one gardener is the allocation of separate spatial areas, traditionally the matron tending ornamentals while the man of the house raises fruits and vegetables. Of course, there may be a bit of cross-border sniping every once in a while: "How many zucchinis do you think we can possibly eat in one year?" or "Surely you're not going to combine pink musk mallows with those lovely red roses!" But, as anachronistic as this scheme seems, it works surprisingly well at providing small empires of independence to the various players.

Alternatively, the work in an undivided garden may be parcelled out by way of job description, ideally dictated by the various skills and interests of those involved—"I'm good at pruning and you're a terrific weeder, so let's get on with it." Ah, but not so fast! The real trick here is not about claiming the chores you want to do, but rather avoiding the ones you don't. Like hand-picking scores of pear-slug larvae off pear-tree leaves. Parameters must be firmly set and stoutly defended or you'll end up doing all the dirty work and getting none of the thanks.

In some households the question arises of how to also get the kids productively engaged in the garden. This is not a field in which I have any experience, and just as well for the hypothetical kids who might have been involved had fate not treated them more kindly. Many of today's enlightened gardening parents appear to take an upbeat "isn't this fun?" approach to getting the wee ones into harness, whereas I likely would have assigned them the dirtiest work available as a matter of grim duty and character building. Come to think of it, a couple of little nippers might have proven quite handy for plucking off those filthy pear slugs.

Any which way you slice it, there are some rocky roads to be ridden in the months ahead and perhaps fearsome retributions to be faced for work undone ("You said you were going to transplant the darn things last week!" "I most certainly did not. I specifically asked you to!") or poorly done ("Oh, for heaven's sake, I should have just done it myself!"). Fibs may be told, tempers lost, wily stratagems employed and power struggles elongated long into the growing season.

But all this too will pass once the gardens burgeon into their full flourishing, credit being given and taken wherever credit is due, and everyone left wondering in hindsight just what all the fuss was about.

Shear Drama

AMONG THE MULTITUDE of tasks required in a garden, I enjoy few as thoroughly as the clipping of shrubs. Digging, planting, weeding, watering—each may appeal in its own way, for a limited time at least, but seldom does any of them sustain an illumination of spirit in the way that clipping does. The simple act of addressing a shaggy hedge or fuzzy specimen shrub and shearing it into a tight and shiny excellence entails an element of artistry, an intense engagement with shapes and surfaces, with textures, contours and contrasts that is both enlivening in the doing and gratifying in the final product.

The inherent complication with clipped shrubs is that they're so appealing, the besotted gardener tends to keep adding more and more of them to the landscape. What began for us as a modest collection of variegated hollies, huckleberries and dwarf spruce systematically expanded over the years to include gangs of boisterous mahonias, English and Portugal laurels, somber yews and cryptomerias, supplementary spruce, along with junipers, cypress, mugo pines, smatterings of chamaecyparis, berberis and daphne, a row of excessively ambitious aucuba, an insurrection of photinia and a truly reckless expanse of boxwood, both Korean and English.

Throughout this epoch of shrub expansionism, I had remained faithful to my tried-and-true tools: a pair of ancient wooden-handled garden shears for the heavier going, supplemented with steel sheep-shears for more delicate trimming. The dextrous wielding of these old implements, the gratifying snip-snip of their scissoring blades, the gentle cascade of severed twig tips, the subtle beauties of form and texture achieved, together elevated what in other circumstances might have been a tiresome chore into the loftier realm of esthetic endeavour. But over time the sweet delight of shearing began to fall under siege from the sheer demands of the expanding shrubbery; for as delightful as a meticulously clipped hedge may be, an unkempt hedge quickly becomes a vexation, hinting as it does at unfulfilled ambition. Plus, some of the more exuberant shrubs—here I'm thinking of photinias and laurels especially—became so tall I had to balance on a wobbly stepladder in order to reach their upper limits.

Around this time, an electric hedge trimmer fell into my possession and I took it into the garden to test its merits, going after a particularly muscular *Mahonia aquifolium* whose dense and prickly foliage was always a challenge to my old clippers. Now within minutes, under the insistent scissoring of the electric hedger, the whole rough surface of it was sliced with scientific precision. The downside of this miracle tool was that it entailed dragging along behind it an enormous stretch of extension cord that would manage to get itself snagged on or wrapped around every possibility. And I was ever alert to the imagined hazards of my slicing the line with the trimmer and getting jolted with 120 volts for my carelessness. I soon realized that, although the tool certainly made short work of the job, something precious was lost in the process.

So I took what was for me an uncharacteristically bold step. Having watched professional hedge trimmers at work—being especially impressed at Powis Castle in Wales, where it takes a staff of four workers three months to clip all the magnificent yews once a year—I determined to buy, expense be damned, a gasoline-powered hedge cutter with an extended drive tube that would allow me to shear with ease well above my own height and without the treacherous stepladder or confounded electric cord. Yes, I know, I know—this involves burning fossil fuel, albeit sparingly, as well as adding more decibels to the industrial noise of our soundscape. But the joy of proceeding around the homestead and accomplishing in a few hours what had previously involved days of laborious hand clipping has muted the worst of my misgivings.

There is, however, I believe, a perverse inclination among devoted clipping people to repeatedly exceed the capacity of whatever technologies are at hand for the work. No sooner had I got things more or less under control with the power hedger than I started up a new scheme for shearing young Douglas fir trees. Dozens of these keep springing up in places where a big conifer wouldn't work but a nicely sheared evergreen shrub certainly would. The long-range thinking here is that once we've passed on into the great shrubbery beyond, these temporarily suppressed trees will be released to grow naturally into the mighty conifers they're designed to become. Keeping them clipped for now seems preferable to removing them entirely.

Meanwhile, with the super-hedger maintaining these juveniles and the outlying big shrubs in shape, I've been freed up (almost) to spend as many hours as I choose delicately clipping by hand the more civilized shrubs in the garden. The process is rather like the old story about painting the Brooklyn Bridge—that by the time the painters get to the end, it's necessary to go back to the other end and start all over again. Indeed, I was forewarned not long ago by a concerned observer that our plan to move toward a less labour-intensive garden by replacing other plantings with carefree shrubbery was utter folly because the endless clipping would eventually do us in. Quite possibly so, but I try not to think about it. In the interim, I'm experiencing anew, as in the Arcadian bliss of early days, that sense of contemplative artistry that every dedicated clipper wants a cut of.

The Ace of Spades

AFTER A VERY frustrating morning of attempting—and failing—to solve a problem existing somewhere off in the Ethernet, I fled outdoors for a session of therapeutic spading. Like fine music or good wine, spading has near-magical properties able to soothe jangled nerves and restore the distraught to equanimity. I'm not sure that society at large wouldn't be considerably less wound up if more of the population practised therapeutic digging.

Some gardeners prefer using a rototiller to turn their soil, an approach I attempted once earlier in life, but finding it such a noisome and bone-jarring experience—and such an assault on the earthworms and their allies—I elected never to repeat it. Other growers choose to harrow their ground as little as possible, opting instead for a permanent-mulch, no-dig regime, an eminently correct and labour-saving option, once the earth has been fully cleared of roots and rocks and brought to reasonable tilth. Both those systems have their advantages, but at considerable cost, for neither offers the same physical intimacy with the soil that manual spading does. Nor, unless I'm quite mistaken, can either calm the spirit with the restorative vigour of spading.

On the afternoon in question, I decided to dig over a new bed for potatoes. The vegetable patch is generally preferred for unfettered spading, as whole beds can be turned without the caution required in ornamental beds where hidden bulbs or roots may be sliced disastrously by the spade. With few such hazards in the potager, the mind is free to wander, the spirit to soar, while the body does its earthy work.

I use a sturdy, long-handled spade, theoretically with its blade filed sharp—a sharp blade, as the old adage goes, being half the work of spading—and wear my heaviest leather workboots. The plunge of the boot-driven spade into soil (straight down, not at a half-hearted angle), the levering back of the spade handle, the rhythmic bending of knees and turning over of the clod, the smacking with spade blade to break it apart—these are the time-honoured elements of a ritual that reaches down to the heart of our relationship with earth.

There's that distinctive aroma, fine as the smell of fresh-brewed coffee, which only soil newly turned in spring gives off. It's a smell that's impossible to describe, but it's unmistakable and readily discernible from similar aromas, say of compost or leaf mould. Like sodbusters of old, I like to take up a handful of soil, smell it and sift it through my fingers, noting its particles and the attenuated filaments threading among them.

Spading again, I watch disgruntled ground beetles, centipedes, millipedes and sowbugs scurry off to escape the disturbance. Indeed, a solid argument against spading can be made on the grounds that it unduly disturbs all of the life forms at work in the earth, including the magical mushrooms already mentioned. Nevertheless, several flimsy justifications can be advanced in favour of sustained spading. One is the requirement that pernicious weeds, along with random potatoes, carrots and such from the previous year, be unearthed and taken away. Another is the need to continuously remove stones from our soil. Although I've dug these beds for decades, each time carting off buckets of stones, there are always more pebbles and rocks awaiting. But I'm happy to have them, if for no other reason than as a justification for spading. Plus, I like the notion that chemical decomposition is endlessly at work breaking stone down into soil, just as biological decomposition is occurring in organic matter.

Great diggers in their own right, earthworms live at the intersection of these twin processes. They harvest scraps of partly decomposed organic debris from the surface and pull them underground, where they consume the stuff, along with mineral particles. Their relentless digging is prodigious: Charles Darwin calculated in a slow moment that earthworms working in one acre of good earth will move up to eighteen tons of soil in a year, aerating the ground in the process. The castings they leave behind are a rich mix of organic and mineral elements that have passed through each worm's digestive tract. In part to encourage worm activity, I spread a surface mulch of grass clippings or leaves over the vegetable beds in autumn. When I spade the beds over in spring, plowing in the remains of the mulch, I see scores of pink, plump worms worming around in the soil.

What you can't see are the billions of other organisms active in good garden loam—just one handful is said to contain more living organisms than there are humans on the planet. These are the masses of fungi, bacteria, protozoa and other micro-organisms that cluster around and feed upon scraps of decaying vegetation. Working together in complex disassembly lines, they break down plant tissues into constituent elements that can ultimately be absorbed by living plants. It's a process of such energetic frenzy that one observer described it as "bacterial fires in the soil."

For the fires to keep burning, the soil must be warm (at least fifteen degrees Celsius), moist, well aerated and neither too acidic nor too alkaline. There must be abundant organic matter for the micro-organisms to feed on, but not so much that the decomposers seize all available nutrients to support their own burgeoning populations, thereby depriving growing plants. This is why adding compost is so useful, because much of the preliminary decomposition has already occurred in the heap.

Conscious of the universe of seething organisms underfoot and of one's own modest role as assistant in the great and ancient work of soil building, a person can spade away contentedly for a good long while—spine, joints and muscles permitting—as vexations snarling from the Ethernet or other sources slowly decompose and melt away.

PUTTING IT ON THE TABLE

Mulch Ado about Everything

THE SIMPLE TRUTH that vegetable gardening requires keeping the soil uniformly moist and free of weeds became evident when Sandy and I first set down roots on our island acreage four decades ago. Tenacious thistles, brambles, bracken fern and other tough customers were constantly seeking a toehold in the large vegetable patch we'd scratched out of the logging slash. The only source of water—upon which life itself depended—was a shallow excavation in a swampy area. A cantankerous gas-fired pump delivered the water with more noise than reliability, and in summer the well was quickly pumped dry.

In these desperate circumstances we soon learned the true and beautiful benefits of mulch. We owned a tattered paperback titled *Gardening without Work* and written by the great maven of mulch, Ruth Stout. In those days, she seemed like a lone voice in the wilderness, but her voice rang true in our wilderness of weeds and parched earth. We began mulching with anything we could get our hands on—spoiled hay, seaweed, even huge skunk-cabbage leaves, anything to clothe the bare earth.

Eventually, two technological breakthroughs helped enormously: the demands of recycling decreed that newspapers be printed with non-toxic inks, and our estate acquired an old rotary lawn mower that could efficiently catch clippings from the extensive grassy areas. Newspapers and grass clippings together formed the backbone of a brilliant mulching system that saved us from perpetual weeding, as well as from drought and desiccation. We used grass clippings to mulch roses, delphiniums, hostas and other moisture-lovers in the ornamental gardens, but the system achieved its fullest flowering in the vegetable garden. Here's how it worked: the veggie patch is divided into oblong raised beds running north-south, each about one and a half metres wide, allowing easy access from either side. The beds and pathways between them are permanent, so compost and other amendments are always added to the growing area, not to places destined to be pathways next year. We don't use any fixed edging along the beds, but simply slope the soil up, eliminating niches for weeds, slugs and sowbugs. In spring, after I'd dug the beds over, added compost, raked them level and planted them, I'd spread a fresh layer of newspapers all along the paths and going up the sloping sides of the beds. We'd gather the papers all winter from the general store and from friends who'd save them for us. Glossy magazines with coloured pictures were not acceptable, as those inks contain elements you don't want in your soil.

Damp newspapers worked best, as they could be moulded to shape on the paths. Besides being prone to blowing away in spring winds, dry copies had the disadvantage of offering readable stories I may have missed earlier, and a lot of time could be squandered scanning the gossip columns rather than getting on with mulching. The papers were laid much like shingles on a roof, carefully overlapped, and always with the folded edge exposed, to prevent the wind from getting into them. Any small stones unearthed during digging could be scattered along the papered paths to help hold the papers in place. Once the soil had warmed up and emerging plants were a few centimetres high, I'd mulch the beds with grass clippings, lapping them over the top edge of the papers. As time went by, I'd apply additional layers of clippings and by the end of May, when the garden was fully planted, no bare earth could be seen anywhere—all the paths were under paper and all the beds under grass.

The system's advantages were undeniable. Virtually all weeds were suppressed and the time saved from not having to constantly pull them out soon surpassed the time initially spent laying down the mulch. Moisture retention under the mulch was remarkable; wherever I would pull back a bit of it, the soil below would feel gorgeously cool and moist throughout. Perfect for plants that prefer uniform moistness rather than a fluctuating cycle of drying out and re-soaking. And the mulch layer seethed with life. Earthworms, of course, thrived under there, as did ground beetles, centipedes and other predators. Enormous populations of hunting spiders roamed through the mulch, presumably pouncing on pest insects. Garter snakes lived in there too—we'd often see one of these sleek beauties emerge from inside the mulch layer or slither gently into it for cover or to hunt slugs, grubs or other pests. The mulch layer, by imitating nature, played a key role in establishing a more ecological balance in the admittedly contrived environment of the vegetable patch. The ultimate goal, as Ruth Stout told us long ago, is a permanent mulch layer that is repeatedly topped up and beneath which a rich and fertile loam awaits the pulling back of mulch and dropping in of seed or transplant.

Alas, as other best-laid schemes gang aft agley, so did this one. Two unforeseen circumstances conspired to undermine what had seemed a superb system. First, the availability of newspapers plunged dramatically when the general store no longer set out big piles of unsold papers every morning. A good thing, of course, in the larger picture, but a loss on the local level. Far worse was the coming of the coons that I've already lamented. Searching for grubs and worms under the mulch, they'd excavate whole beds and ruin everything in the process. They'd pull the newspapers apart, leaving them to dry out and scatter in the wind. What had once been the epitome of cultivated mulching was degraded to an infuriating mess.

Nowadays our mulching is a shadow of its former glory. Any plantings that are protected—strawberry beds under nets and carrots under Remay cloth—still benefit from a thick grass mulch. So do the squash hills, with old fishnet spread across the mulch and anchored with heavy stones. Peppers, aubergines and tomatoes inside the greenhouses all are heavily mulched. But overall it's a pallid affair compared with what once was. Of course, times are not as desperate as they were: after decades of soil building, the ground is far more retentive of moisture than the dust and stones of the early days. Plus, there's now abundant water available from a deep well. But persistent weeds like creeping buttercup and sheep sorrel push in wherever the earth lies bare, giving rise to extra weeding as well as to fond remembrance of times past when the earth was fully clothed in mulch.

Now, Who Wants to Volunteer?

VOLUNTEERISM IS THE lifeblood of any thriving community. Hordes of energetic volunteers bustling about to lend a helping hand with fighting fires, coaching hockey, caring for the elderly, saving wildlife habitat, and numerous other worthy causes—they're a noble breed and true antidote to the "me first" narcissism prevalent in darker corners of society.

Similarly, volunteerism among plants brings vitality and a welcome insouciance into the garden, and most particularly into the vegetable patch. This is true for all the growing seasons, but never more so than in spring when a half-dozen or more types of robust volunteers germinate unbidden in the warming soil. At our place, we welcome these cooperative characters as vital links in the early-season food chain. And, at a time of year when gardening workaholism is at a fever pitch, it's especially gratifying to hitch a free ride on the backs of low-maintenance volunteers, bestowing as they do a brief illusion that the days ahead will be marked by serendipity rather than by blisters.

I'm not including here stolid springtime perennials such as sorrel and chives, nor spring's gastronomical "weeds" like chickweed and stinging nettle, but rather domesticated varieties with a penchant for going their own merry way in the garden, independent of our ministrations.

Chervil, *Anthriscus cerefolium,* a free-seeding annual that thrives in cool weather, is one of them. The smart set call it "gourmet's parsley" because of its ferny little leaves with an upscale taste of anise. I like John Evelyn's description from the seventeenth century: "The tender tips of chervil should never be wanting in our sallets, being exceedingly wholesome and cheering of the spirits." If you're so inclined, you can sow chervil seeds in well-tilled soil, thin the plants to fifteen centimetres and provide them with winter protection. We don't bother. Instead, I just leave a few plants growing along the pathways to seed where they will. Early every spring, there's a nice little crop for spicing up the salad bowl and cheering the spirits.

Parsley's much the same. I've long ago ceased seeding it, as this biennial suffers from a serious excess of enthusiasm in the matter of self-seeding. It's essential to remove most flowering stems before they set seed unless you want a parsley farm. I like to confine it to the northern edges of raised beds, though confinement is not in *Petroselinum crispum*'s game plan. We grow both the curly and flat-leaved, or Italian, type, and continue cutting their vitamin- and mineral-rich leaves from early spring until well into winter. It's rather disingenuous to say we "grow" it, as we do virtually nothing except ensure that creeping buttercup, a pernicious weed that somewhat resembles parsley in appearance, doesn't insinuate itself into the parsley patch.

Corn salad, *Valerianella olitoria*, is far less indiscriminate both in its seeding regime and the time span of its availability. Known as lamb's lettuce, this dainty annual produces small rosettes of leaves with a lovely sweet, nutty taste. Seeds from springtime plants will germinate and grow in the fall and often overwinter outdoors. Where parsley requires a firm hand and occasional eviction, little corn salad modestly confines her self-seeding to a quite small area.

The same is true of orach, *Atriplex hortensis*. Often called red spinach, mountain spinach or giant lambsquarters, this native of western Asia and the Mediterranean region produces red, greenish or yellowish triangular leaves that make a healthy and colourful contribution to the mid-spring salad bowl. It's touted as an alternative to spinach, and there are few annuals I'd rather have an alternative to. Spinach cannot, will not, does not grow for me. I've tried everything short of bloodletting, but the damn stuff simply refuses to cooperate. Orach, meanwhile, pops up on its own, grows vigorously without any assistance, tolerates both heat and cold and doesn't bolt to seed overnight the way spinach would...if it were to grow at all. Repeated failure in the spinach bed remains a humiliation, but one made tolerable by the good graces of orach. Eventually its flowering stalk will grow to about two metres tall, producing hordes of husks, each of which contains a single seed. Deeply appreciative, we leave a few of these attractive plants to cast seeds for next spring.

I do the same with cilantro, *Coriandrum sativum*, also known as Chinese parsley. Its tasty leaves, once they've worked their way into your cuisine, are highly addictive and it becomes impossible to ever have too much cilantro. Only the larger early leaves possess the desired rich flavour, so diligent cropping and a constant supply of new plants is in order.

Invariably, those I cultivate from seed thrive far less well than do successive generations of volunteers.

This is true of the other springtime volunteers as well. They've plainly got some hankering for independence, doing best when they're free to hopscotch around the veggie patch and put down their temporary roots wherever they will. I think of them as having an RV-lifestyle attitude. You see the same pattern in their summertime successors: the dill, 'Red Russian' kale and borage who'll loll around in spots of their own choosing a bit later in the season.

It's a delicate balancing act to manage a garden that accommodates these desirable upstarts while preventing rank anarchy from seizing the ground and overwhelming it with unruly jungle. But I like the creative give-and-take of combining the capricious with the methodical. Carrots or rutabagas in regimental rows are immensely gratifying in their own stolid way, but not to the exclusion of those nearby vagabonds, the carefree volunteers.

Stalk Investments

EVERY SO OFTEN a particular garden project demands a horticultural full-frontal assault in which tremendous resources and huge reserves of energy must be expended. Creating an asparagus bed—at least doing so on our stony ground—is just such a project. Our first stab at asparagus cultivation, many years ago, was such an incontrovertible failure—extremely modest harvests soon declined into a melancholy dwindling away of the plants—it discouraged further attempts. Fellow gardeners reported similarly dismal histories. As Oregon garden-writer Steve Solomon put it in *Growing Vegetables West of the Cascades:* "On our side of the mountains, keeping an asparagus patch alive over winter can be dicey—the winter is virtually impossible on heavy, slow-draining soils. In drier microclimates and on deep, light loam soils, asparagus may not be too difficult. Perhaps."

But no crop is more rewarding, timelier or more essentially correct than a well-grown bed of asparagus. And thus it came to pass that we decided to attempt the impossible again.

Asparagus plants are usually acquired by purchasing two-year-old roots at a garden centre, but heeding the advice of a favourite seed catalogue that "varieties grown from seed have many desirable characteristics," I ordered seeds of 'Jersey Knight', all-male plants with a high tolerance to fusarium wilt, crown rot and rust. Slightly disconcerted by the paucity of seeds in the pricey package, I planted them in small pots in the glass house in spring and was gratified by robust germination. In May I lined the little plants out in a holding bed in the vegetable garden.

Then the real work—preparing the bed itself—began. Because asparagus plants should continue yielding abundant crops for many years, getting the soil properly prepared at the outset is of the essence. I selected a bed about one metre wide by six metres long at the perimeter of the garden, away from the hurly-burly of annual cropping. I started out by "bastard-trenching," a manic undertaking favoured by old English gardeners who have lost all sense of perspective. It involves excavating a trench across one end of the bed, moving that topsoil to its opposite end, breaking up the subsoil in the excavated trench to the depth of a "spit" (the length of a spade blade), filling the trench with topsoil from a second trench excavated immediately adjoining the first, and repeating the sequence until the whole bed has been trenched. This was a slow process, with wheelbarrow-loads of rocks, gravel and old tree roots being hauled away, and much in the way of sore muscles, aching back and general self-condolence.

Because asparagus roots prefer more than a metre of open soil through which to descend, I set about raising the bed well above ground level. Some sheets of old metal roofing, cut down the middle, offered a rot-resistant edging of sufficient height, back-stopped by yellow cedar stakes. This left us with what looked like an Olympic-sized swimming pool needing to be filled with perfect soil. No problem.

First, I lugged out from the forest about thirty big bucketsful of duff sloughed off an ancient Douglas fir snag. Next, I added homemade compost and leaf mould. Reluctantly, I bought four bales of peat moss and worked them in. I balanced their acidity with buckets of wood ash saved from the wood stove over winter. By this point, the pit was filling handsomely.

Then came the luxury ingredients. We'd been given an enormous truckload—some fourteen cubic metres—of Sea Soil, a splendid compost derived from forest fines and salmon waste. In the past I've been reluctant to use salmon-based compost in the veggie garden for fear of contaminants. However, this particular product has been approved and certified for all levels of organic production, and so with as clear a conscience as one can achieve nowadays, I wheelbarrowed load after load of this black gold to the new bed.

Next, I added a bag of glacial rock dust, a slow-release, broad-spectrum mineral product that helps improve soil structure, nutrient availability and bacterial action. In the trenches into which the roots were to be set, I worked in an all-purpose organic fertilizer. Lastly, as I set the precious roots into the trenches, I inoculated each root with a teaspoon of the mycorrhizal fungus *Glomus intraradices,* which works in a symbiotic relationship with perennial plants, enhancing their capacity to absorb nutrients from soil. In short, like a pork-barrelling politician facing re-election, I threw every conceivable resource into that asparagus bed. No area in our gardens has ever been prepared with such diligence, lavished with such high-end amendments. If there's any justice in this world, we concluded, this would indeed be an asparagus bed for the ages.

And so, for a while, it appeared to be. By their third season, the plants bristled with spears so stout and succulent we were able to indulge in asparagus at will. With the possible exception of steamed nettles, no taste more perfectly distills the essence of spring. We had accomplished what so many before us had attempted but failed to do. A whiff of self-congratulation accompanied every perusal of the lustily thrusting spears. I imagined myself in the company of those old codgers in the Maritimes who every autumn astound the whole country with their impossibly oversized pumpkins.

However, one particular problem can bedevil an asparagus patch: the intrusion of female plants. As mentioned, I'd originally started with a package of male-only seeds. But, as not mentioned, we fell a bit short on plants, and I had subsequently germinated another pack of ungendered seeds, well over half of which eventually turned out to be female. This became apparent once they started producing bright-red seed pods in autumn. Female plants are frowned upon both because their shoots are allegedly less robust than male spears and because their seeds germinate into multiple new plants that have to be continually weeded out to prevent crowding of the original roots.

I tried my best in this regard, flagging all the female plants with surveyor's tape and cutting the female tops off before the seeds could ripen. At first I thought I'd dig them out, giving the male plants room to stretch out and have the bed to themselves. Then, instead, I decided to simply continue gathering the female spears well beyond the standard one-month harvest time, thereby getting more shoots to eat while at the same time weakening the unwanted females. This struck me as a clever but disturbingly patriarchal approach. On further reflection, I began wondering whether a bed of exclusively male plants would truly be a happy place in the long haul. While I dithered on the horns of ethical dilemma, the females got about doing what females do: procreating.

Within a couple of years, all the plants of whatever gender were plainly losing vigour, declining into the flaccid little failures we'd produced in earlier attempts. Eventually I excavated the bed, finding an uproar of roots strangling one another. I thought to tear them all out and replant the best of them, but which were male and which female? Then

I discovered the roots can't be successfully moved after their first few years. We had on our hands an outlandish pile of entirely useless roots.

Some people might give up after such an odyssey of ineptitude, buy the occasional bundle of spears at the farmers' market and call it a day. Not us. We recharged the bed with nutrients and started a new set of plants from seed. We've yet to cut a single spear, but remain convinced that this might yet prove to be an asparagus bed for the ages.

Broad Appeal

OF ALL THE satisfactions to be savoured in the early-summer garden, none surpasses the immense sense of well-being engendered by a thriving bed of broad beans. Quickly out of the gate, stout of stem, succulent of leaf, the very embodiment of vegetative vigour, at this time of year the broad bean almost single-handedly bids the gardener set aside all anxiety about successful crops in the season to come. Long before other beans can even be planted in the slowly warming earth, weeks before tomatoes or squash or aubergines can be coaxed from their sheltered quarters for a few timid hours during the warmth of the day, flowering broad beans are already giving promise of a bountiful harvest.

It's this characteristic robustness that encourages enthusiasts to continue calling them broad beans rather than fava beans, as Americans do. They (the beans, not the Americans) have a broad-shouldered Paul Bunyanesque quality that fava (from the Italian for *Vicia faba*) doesn't quite capture. Broad beans: Simple. Blunt. Blue collar. For the same reason, we stick with the classic variety 'Broad Windsor Long Pod'. Over the years, we've flirted with loftier varieties—reputed to have softer skin and more delicate flesh—but have yet to be smitten by any of them. We're now having a dalliance with a couple of newer varieties from Salt Spring Seeds. We shall see.

I plant our seed—saved from the best of the previous year's pods—after the warm spell that invariably occurs in February. In earlier times, I planted in late fall, but several winters of extreme cold succeeded in blackening and killing the new shoots, so now I wait until the worst of the heavy weather is past. I plant four parallel rows in a bed roughly one and a half by six metres long, and then spread a floating row cover over the plantings. The cover is intended partly to help raise the soil temperature a few degrees, but also to hide the emerging plants from thieves. I began employing this defensive measure because one season we had magnificent germination, then went away for a short time and returned to find that every single bean sprout had disappeared, neatly plucked from the soil so as to leave rows of small but vacant holes. I had no shred of evidence, but was perfectly prepared to blame raccoons for this grand larceny, until a colleague advanced a convincing argument that song sparrows were a more likely culprit. Upon reflection, I had to concede that the beans had been plucked daintily from the earth without any raccoonish mayhem.

With foul weather and thieves outwitted, the bean plants burgeon through late winter and early spring. By the time they're a foot or so high, I drive stout stakes along the rows and attach several flights of twine to hold the plants upright. Frequently reaching two metres high and weighted with heavy pods, unsupported plants have a propensity for toppling in wind and rain. Some people are plagued with aphids attacking the tender new shoots, but this is not an issue for us. Otherwise trouble-free, they're a reliable cool-weather crop, producing bountifully in locations that are not balmy enough for long enough to sustain other bean types.

The essence of broad-bean cuisine is to begin eating them fresh as soon as possible. We devour the young beans throughout early summer, most frequently parboiled and then quick-fried in olive oil with thinly sliced garlic and a pinch of salt. But the mountainous crop soon outstrips our ability to consume them. Some we dry for use in next winter's soups. Others get pureed with garlic and then frozen for later use in spreads, dips and hummus, as well as a replacement for refried beans in burritos. I value all the other beans we grow, but none sustains us throughout the following winter as generously as this bountiful and healthful bean, rich in protein, iron and potassium.

Given their ease of cultivation and their many culinary uses, why do broad beans receive such a bad rap in certain quarters? In the sixth century BC the Greek philosopher and mathematician Pythagoras (he of the squared hypotenuse) warned his followers to "avoid fava beans." Later on, Aristotle theorized that Pythagoras's problem with favas could be explained in part "because they have the shape of testicles." Just what this comment implies about either of these deep Greek thinkers might make for robust speculation in institutes of higher learning. Diogenes in turn focused his philosophical cynicism upon what's called the flatulence factor: "One should abstain from fava beans, since they are full of wind and take part in the soul, and if one abstains from them one's stomach will be less noisy and one's dreams will be less oppressive and calmer."

The same might well be said about abstaining from philosophy, but that's a separate discussion. Suffice it to say that the old Greek scholars were actually on to something, because certain people do in fact suffer from a genetic condition called favism that can trigger severe reactions, including death, from eating fresh broad beans. More common in males than females, the responsible blood-enzyme deficiency is found primarily in genetic pools originating in the Mediterranean area.

Anyone suffering from favism is naturally excused from unbridled enthusiasm for broad beans. But as for the rest of us, no rationale—noisy stomachs or oppressive dreams or testicle aversions—seems capable of diminishing our loyalty to this versatile broad-shouldered workhorse of the vegetable patch.

The Polyester Potager

WE TAKE GREAT pride at our place in having things look as "natural" as possible—hydro lines buried, vehicles parked out of sight, appurtenances fashioned from wood or stone wherever possible, no inconvenience too great in the service of natural cool. And nowhere more so than in the vegetable patch. Fenced with hand-split cedar rails, our potager sports more rustic touches than a cheesy Alberta dude ranch. But even in this bastion of organic aspirations, the products of industrialism are making steady headway, most notoriously the extensive sheaths of garden fabric that now blanket many beds. Although naturalistically referred to as "floating row covers," these products are the very essence of synthetic, formed from spunbonded polyester or polyethylene, so that encountering sheets of them stretched in every direction conjures the impression of an ersatz garden swathed in unwholesome fabrication.

But, my goodness, the stuff comes in handy. I use a heavyweight row cover first off to protect the earliest outdoor plantings of arugula, lettuce et al. The advantages here are twofold: it can boost soil temperature and offer protection from late frosts, while also deterring pilferers. Raccoons, for example. A creature of extraordinary cunning, as previously lamented, the raccoon is for some reason entirely dumbfounded by a sheet of garden fabric. We'll frequently see their muddy little paw prints on top of the fabric, but they'll not have figured out they could easily lift the cloth and set about the digging they'd certainly do if it wasn't there. Or perhaps the polyesterishness of the stuff is offensive to their refined sensibilities and they prefer to ignore it entirely.

If early-spring crop protection were the fabric's sole raison d'être, and the material could be folded up and removed from sight prior to the full leafy glories of springtime, all might be well. But that's not the case, because floating row cover next offers one of its greatest benefits: the exclusion of flying insect pests. In fact, I began my unseemly affair with garden fabric in a last-gasp bid to outwit the carrot rust fly, the unlovely *Psila rosae*, whose tunnelling larvae were rendering our carrots unfit for human consumption. I'd tried a number of ineffective preventative measures, including a mulch of used coffee grounds from the local café, without success. The fly continued to lay her eggs alongside our carrots and the resultant grubs persisted in their entirely natural but to us disgusting tunnelling. A floating row cover promised the possibility of an insect barrier, preventing the fly from getting to the carrots in the first place.

To be effective, however, the fabric edges must offer not even the slightest gap through which the maternal fly might slip. One method is to tuck the fabric into the soil all along the bed; another is to pin the fabric to the soil with galvanized wire staples. Both work wonderfully, so long as there's no requirement to regularly check what's going on under the covers. But periodic peeking beneath the sheets is highly recommended. I found that out with a bed of beets I'd covered to prevent the leafminer fly from setting her dislikeable offspring tunnelling through the beet leaves. I'd secured the fabric with a series of small boulders that could be readily removed at inspection time. For several weeks, I regularly lifted the fabric at one corner of the bed and was delighted to see robust little beets growing in abundance. But when I eventually pulled the whole fabric away to give the young plants a first thinning, I discovered to my dismay that the bed contained only that one small corner of good growth, the remainder being thinly populated with spotty stragglers hardly worth protecting and certainly not needing any thinning.

Other mishaps await. As the weather warms, protection from insects is best achieved using lightweight or summer-weight fabric, which allows in more sunlight and traps less heat. But, having fastidiously covered the bed with heavier fabric early on, it's easy to postpone replacing the cover with more lightweight material. On one such occasion I managed to roast an entire bed of young carrots left under heavy cover during a sudden heat wave. Another time, the excessive heat apparently provoked a good percentage of carrots to bolt to seed a full year ahead of schedule.

Overheating can be in part ameliorated by having the fabric stretched over hoops or other devices to keep it well above the vegetation level. This is the juncture at which one realizes that the fabric isn't sufficiently wide to both straddle the hoops and reach the sides of the bed. Then the wind kicks up and pretty soon there are great banners of cloth flapping about the garden like pennants on the crowded grounds of a transformative festival. For carrots at least, I've refined my technique so that the fabric forms a low wall around the perimeter of the bed, sufficiently high to deter the female rust fly because it travels in a ground-hugging flight pattern, but leaving the carrots open to the sky as they plainly prefer to be. Hope is on the horizon that new fine-mesh netting developed specifically for pest prevention will soon be readily available.

Meanwhile, floating row cover is theoretically good for two or three seasons, if it's carefully dried and stored away from moisture and sunlight. However, even one small rent or tear will render it useless for insect protection, although damaged cloth can still be used to help keep the frosts off. My experience has been that the lighter, summer-weight material frequently doesn't make it through even its first season. For the rest, I tend to reuse our pieces until they've disintegrated into unseemly tatters. By the end of the season, the entire garden, organic or not, resembles a failed attempt at aping one of the artist Christo's gigantic wrapped installations, like the one that surrounded eleven islands in Miami's Biscayne Bay with six hundred thousand square metres of pink polypropylene floating fabric.

No, it's not rustic and it's certainly not natural, but it keeps the damn leafminer and rust fly out, and that's good enough for me.

Sticks and Stones

EVERYONE OF GOOD sense recognizes the gardener's genius with seeds, slips and secateurs; but do we acknowledge her equally essential expertise with sticks and stones? Throughout the growing season, the garden is a marvel of inventiveness in all manner of propping up and weighing down, mostly involving those elemental implements, sticks and stones.

There can never be too many sticks in a garden. There's the obvious bamboo canes for staking delphiniums or stout cedar stakes for holding up tomato vines, but also refinements involving odd little sticks for supporting weak-kneed oriental poppies or yarrow, twisted sticks and forked branches for propping up sagging hydrangea limbs. Sticks from which to construct tripods for perennial sweet pea to clamber up. Or clever bits of stick for supporting espaliered peaches under the eaves. A raised bed of broad beans, four rows abreast, each six metres long, four sticks to the row, the robust plants held neatly between twin parallel lines of twine stretched from stake to stake—what joy! What finesse!

A well-stocked stick stash requires that you store sticks all over the place on the perfectly reasonable supposition that on any given day you're going to need at least one. But stick stocking is an art unto itself and an abundance of sticks does not necessarily ensure that you've got the proper stick for the job at hand. Sticks can have an annoying capacity to be either too short or too long for what is required of them. A stick sticking above the head of a plant it's supporting, or a stalk bent over an undersized stick, are both evidence of regrettable stick deficiency. When a stick is longer than required, the imprudent staker cuts it down to size, failing to recognize that this eventually results in a surplus of short sticks and a deficit of long ones. The same principles apply with respect to stoutness of a stick. You don't want a great thick club holding up some wispy little plant any more than you want a slender slip of a stick trying to support a heavyweight specimen. Stick sustainability requires that you go search out a stick of appropriate length and thickness, a process that may drag on for hours, depending upon your store of sticks and the fore-sight with which they have been distributed around the yard.

Quality of sticks is crucial too. Few things are more frustrating than to have a perfectly proportioned and perfectly placed stick snap in half because it was cracked to begin with or rotten at the base. I've had several experiences of tomato vines heavy with ripening fruit snapping their supporting sticks and lurching sickeningly toward the earth. No amount of subsequent buttressing and reinforcing can atone for the original sin of a flawed stick. A sentimentalist at heart, the gardener is loath to throw away sticks that have served faithfully for many seasons, but at a certain point every stick has outlived its usefulness and must be discarded.

And this is the great thing about garden stones—they never wear out. While less versatile than sticks, they're vastly more durable. I'm not meaning stone as part of the garden hardscape—retaining walls, steps and all the rest—but rather random stones that loll about until needed. Stones specialize in inertia and that's what makes them so useful for holding stuff down. I try to keep several dozen granite cobbles, ideally about the size of a cantaloupe, in the vegetable patch for holding the edges of floating row covers or for anchoring fishnetting stretched over the strawberries.

If you're doing a bit of propagation by layering ground-level shoots of a shrub or vine, nothing works better than a good heavy stone to hold the rooting shoot in place. And when it comes to pounding in all those ad hoc sticks and stakes, when the sledgehammer's miles away at the moment, a hefty stone is perfectly adequate for the job.

Stones don't wear out—at least, not at a pace to disturb a gardener—but the disconcerting thing about them is how they keep mysteriously disappearing from the yard. Years ago, when we were first breaking ground at our estate-in-the-making, we were up to our ears in stones of all sorts—from omnipresent pebbles to humongous granite blocks. More quarrymen than gardeners, we'd wheelbarrow tons of stone away for use in making driveways or building foundations. Gradually, the stones grew fewer and the soil deeper. Nowadays, while there are still pebbles and rocks aplenty, we're hard pressed to unearth any substantial stones at all. Since stones are so adept at staying put, you'd think a good supply would last forever, but that's not the case. Truth is you can only maintain an adequate supply by constantly replenishing the stock. The damn things simply vanish on a regular basis. You'd almost think there's a stone thief sneaking in by night and making off with the best of our cobbles. It's a melancholy sight to see a gardener dispiritedly searching the grounds and muttering that there's not a decent stone to be found on the place anymore.

Nevertheless, I particularly cherish those occasions when sticks and stones come together in a symbiotic contribution to the garden, when I've got a good thick stake grasped in one hand and a heavy round cobble in the other. Using a stone to pound a stick into the earth is a strangely satisfying act, a primitive re-enactment that carries one back to our most distant ancestors fumbling with the very beginnings of tool using. It was sticks and stones that set our species upon the path to civilization and woe betide the modern gardener caught short of these essential elements.

Ladybug Love

I WAS BEING driven mad by aphids in the greenhouse. The sweet pepper, aubergine, tomato and basil plants were suffering disastrous infestations of little juice suckers and the filthy diseases they transport. Some leaves were covered with sooty black mould growing on the aphids' excreted honeydew, others turning cancerous colours and wilting to death. We were spending increasing amounts of time laboriously washing off leaves and spraying with insecticidal soap, only to have aphids quickly reappear in increasing numbers. This was one of those points at which a person begins reassessing lofty notions about the inherent correctness and beauty of all living things.

The trouble with aphids, as with tribbles, is that they have no sense of limitation. Birth control is as foreign to them as it was to my Irish Catholic forebears. Aphids are born pregnant; indeed, they can have a minuscule secondary embryo already forming inside a more developed embryo. Spectacularly adapted for overpopulation, they were outwitting us at every turn.

Similarly besieged, editor Carol Pope mentioned to me that she'd purchased a quantity of ladybugs and introduced them into her greenhouse with promising results. Desperate times calling as they do for desperate measures, I plunked down fifteen bucks at the local nursery for a little package bullishly labelled "Aphid Destroyer"—two hundred and fifty ladybugs, *Hippodamia convergens,* sufficient to cover ten medium plants or three trees.

Considerable preparation was required before setting the predators loose. First step was to knock the aphid population back by again washing all infected plant parts with insecticidal soap and then rinsing them with fresh water, giving the ladybugs enough breathing time to get up and running. Secondly, as flying away home is something ladybugs are prone to do, all windows and vents needed to be screened in order to prevent a great escape. (Certain persons in the nursery where Carol had purchased her ladybugs advocated spraying them with a sticky soft-drink/ water mixture to glue their wings shut for a week or so, but this seemed to both me and Carol an undignified treatment of an ally from whom much was expected.) Open water containers were removed to avoid any deaths by drowning. Lastly, all the plants were lightly misted.

Throughout these preparations, the ladybugs were kept in semi-dormancy in the refrigerator—but, finally, on a warm evening, the great moment arrived when the woozy aphid destroyers were gently scattered among the plants. My research had led me to believe that, once released, the ravenous ladybugs would immediately pounce upon and begin devouring aphids. Instead, most of them took to enthusiastic copulating. It has to be said that humping ladybugs look inherently ridiculous, and some of them favoured a multiple-partners approach that appeared almost pornographic. It's not surprising that copulation and procreation should occur, but one might expect that a creature traditionally associated with the Virgin Mary would be a little more discreet about it. (Medieval legend had it that European farmers whose crops were being destroyed by insect plagues implored Mary's intercession, which duly arrived in the form of the beetles eventually named for her.) Unseemly or not, the mating game immediately raised hopes about subsequent generations that would prove a match for our exponentially expanding aphid population.

Their carnal lusts sated, the ladybugs launched the anticipated full assault against the aphids and I took to spending an inordinate amount of time observing our little warriors in action and calibrating their accomplishment. An adult ladybug, we're told, will devour about fifty aphids a day. No doubt about it—soon the aphid numbers were beginning to diminish...but so were the ladybug numbers. Despite my preventive measures, some were obviously finding their way out of the greenhouse, just as misgivings were now finding their way back in.

But then the great moment, less than a week after the initial release, when the first ladybug larvae made their appearance. Dark little six-legged creatures, resembling miniature alligators, the larvae spent about three weeks apparently doing nothing except eating aphids, each reportedly consuming about two dozen a day. Some of the first-generation adults were still at work as well, so the aphids were in full rout.

After their three-week orgy, the larvae entered a pupal stage within little cases attached to leaves and stems. Sensing an opportunity, the aphids mounted a resurgence, but in surprisingly few days, the pupal cases split open and adult ladybugs emerged. After drying out and getting their bearings, they joined in the aphid feast and once again the momentum swung to our side.

By summer's end, after several successive generations of ladybugs, we were able to harvest bountiful ripe peppers, aubergines and tomatoes. Most of the ladybugs had by then disappeared, but not all the aphids had.

The following year, we were far more vigilant about washing off any aphids that first appeared and are now committed to a regimen of planting sweet alyssum in the greenhouse and leaving doors and windows open so that hoverflies and other aphid predators will be attracted by its scent. A more sensible approach certainly, but I did enjoy the Sturm und Drang of the great ladybug and aphid battle.

The Birds and the Beasts

FRUIT AND VEGETABLE growers are perhaps the canniest of all gardening tacticians because we're incessantly called upon to outwit pilferers. All manner of bugs, birds and beasts feel entitled to a free lunch from the fruits of our labours, each with a particular genius of thievery.

In our locale, we're mercifully not plagued by flocks of blackbirds, crows or starlings, but innocent-looking American robins and rufous-sided towhees cause more than enough damage. No ripening strawberry, raspberry or blueberry is safe from them, not to mention any poor earthworm caught above ground. When not berry picking, they're excavating soil and mulch, burying or uprooting tiny seedlings in the process.

I've erected large wooden frames around all the berry bushes and at the first sign of ripening we completely encase the berry patches in fishnet, creating an overall effect of depressing imprisonment. With crops like onions and carrots planted in close lines, I lay old wooden boards between the rows to keep the scratchers out. On other beds, I lay swaths of old fishnet or poultry wire—I've even started experimenting with that newfangled plastic netting that looks as though it'll deteriorate within weeks, but doesn't—beneath which seedlings can grow until they're large enough to withstand the unearthers.

Birds aren't the only pests wanting to excavate where I wish they wouldn't. Neighbourhood cats and freebooting raccoons both enjoy digging up any fresh earth or mulch to be messed around, so my ground-level clutter of mesh and planks is meant to discourage them as well.

Raccoons, of course (have I mentioned them already?), are all but indefensible. After a couple of years of having our grapes and figs torn to pieces, I went so far as to buy a trap and bait it repeatedly with marshmallows. But no raccoon was ever dumb enough to get caught in it, which was a great relief to me as I dreaded any of the available options if I'd actually captured one of these master burglars. Although putting tall metal collars around the lower trunks of fruit trees now prevents coons from climbing up to pillage plums, pears and apples, our grape arbour and multistemmed fig tree are easily breached, leaving us with the less than satisfactory tactic of picking the grapes and figs before they've fully ripened. In the matter of coons (and cats, for that matter), I've concluded that a large and snarly dog is the way to go.

Several years ago, I discovered that—despite my metal collars—something was chewing on the apples and pears. It definitely wasn't the work of pileated woodpeckers, who generally wait until later in the season before jackhammering away at the fruit and destroying far more of it than they eat. Then tomatoes ripening on the vine were being gnawed at too. Mice, perhaps? But the damage seemed too extensive for mice. No…it was rats! An unprecedented plague of what are called tree or roof rats. With an exceptionally long tail to aid in climbing, these sly pilferers are extraordinary acrobats able to circumvent any of my corn-pone defences. They first appeared on the island a few years back, then quickly became a widespread menace to gardens and homes. Rumours began circulating about a certain barge tied up at the wharf being the source of this invasion. After a particularly brazen colony of these rodents invaded the house and took to sleeping on our hot-water tank, I started trapping and threatening them with sufficient machismo that they abandoned the premises and haven't returned.

Sometimes one's clever strategies do more harm than good. One spring, as always, I planted out my cabbage, cauliflower and broccoli seedlings with a square piece of building-paper surrounding their base to prevent root maggots. Within a couple of weeks I had some very sick-looking plants. Turns out I'd used heavier than usual paper so the hole through which each stem protruded became too tight and began choking the plant it was supposed to be protecting. Meanwhile, herds of sowbugs were living contentedly in cool moisture under the paper while dining conveniently on the tortured stalks. In recent years I've counterpunched by sprinkling diatomaceous earth around each stem before attaching a paper collar.

I could go on about subversive voles tunnelling toward the Jerusalem artichokes or cabbage moths amid the brassicas, but instead let me tell you a mystifying tale about how last summer hardly any of the pilferers showed up. Strawberries ripened beautifully without any protective netting. When the raspberries, blueberries and tayberries began to ripen, we decided to skip the labour of dragging out heavy nets and see what would happen. Nothing did. We had a bumper crop with hardly a berry lost to birds. No raccoons snuck in to plunder the grapes or figs. Even the rats had abandoned us as surely as they would a sinking ship. It was downright eerie, almost disappointing, not to have the same old adversaries needing to be outwitted. Were they all now deferring to the genius of our defensive measures, taking their thieving ways to greener pastures less stoutly firewalled than ours?

Or will they be back with a vengeance, and our defensive strategies put to the test once again?

Sweet Recollections

THE DAY WE felled the enormous maple behind our veggie patch, I was forcibly reminded of the scene in James Cameron's *Avatar* in which the great Hometree is brought crashing to the ground. Bigleaf maples are like that—massive and muscular, the largest maple in Canada, almost iconic in their colossal gnarled trunks and skyscraping canopy of branches. Still, sadly, they fall short of being truly iconic in the way ancient oaks or banyan trees are. Even in its native Pacific Northwest, *Acer macrophyllum* seems a poor second cousin to the monumental conifers that typify the coastal forests. Often dismissed as "weed trees," they come across as the Toronto Maple Leafs of trees, systemically incapable of real greatness.

Nevertheless, when we had the big specimen—at least thirty metres high and a metre in diameter at the butt—brought down by an expert faller, we did experience a sense of greatness lost. True, this was one of those necessary sacrifices that gardeners are periodically called upon to execute. Located outside the southeast corner of the vegetable garden, the tree had grown into a sizable problem, its canopy casting a deep morning shade across the garden, its aggressive roots infiltrating the veggie beds, its phytotoxicity discouraging nearby berry bushes, and its innumerable seedlings annually popping up all over the garden.

Despite these provocations, we first took remedial actions in order to spare the tree. We hired skilled climbers to lop off the worst of the big branches stretching over the garden. But within a few years the giant had replaced them with vigorous new limbs. This is the thing about bigleaf maples, both their glory and their downfall: that they grow at an astonishing rate. No tree in our neck of the woods goes from seedling to sapling to sizable tree any quicker, not even the speedy red alder. Some of what now look like ancient maples around our clearing were mere striplings when we arrived here forty years ago. The oldest of them, hoary veterans draped in mosses and lichens, even ferns nestled on their lower limbs, are in the eighty- to hundred-year range. They got their opportunity in the open spaces left after the big Douglas firs were logged off a century ago.

While a Douglas fir is still a youngster at a hundred years, the aging maples are already dying. They succumb reluctantly, one topmost branch after another withering and falling away. And in this stage they can become a real menace, hurling big branches down onto rooftops, power lines and vehicles. Once on the ground, the wood rots away with the same rapidity as it grew, and within a few seasons is reduced to soft humus.

But to disparage bigleaf maples as weed trees is to not know them well, for they do have their uses and their moments of true beauty. Their masses of golden-green flowers are one of the great glories of spring on the coast, besides being brilliant both in bouquets and in the salad bowl. Many's the time I've stood transfixed in our veggie patch while wild bees fed on the big maple's flowers in such multitudes they created a tremendous humming high in its canopy.

For a number of years we tapped our big maples for sap and simmered it down on the wood stove for maple syrup. The sap is considerably thinner than that of eastern sugar maples and we'd need to collect about 132 litres of sap to produce not quite 4 litres of syrup. We've milled maple trunks for lumber too, some of which forms a handsome plank floor in our summer house. In certain places it's highly prized for instrument and furniture making, and near the southern end of its range, in Oregon, you hear of fine woodworkers approaching apoplexy over mature maples being cut up for firewood. We haven't burnt much of it ourselves, although the wood's noted for burning slow and steady and creating glowing embers.

Typically the bigleaf maples' autumn show is decidedly average, particularly by the dazzling standards of their eastern and Japanese cousins, but every so often when conditions are just right, *macrophyllum* decks herself out in a mantle of golden leaves as fine as any in the family. The sound of her big dry leaves cascading to earth is the very essence of autumnal melancholy. One of my favourite fall chores is raking the fallen leaves into piles where they'll eventually rot into usable leaf mould.

I've taken care to nurture and transplant offspring from our felled giant, protecting them with wire cages from deer that readily browse the leaves of young trees, eventually killing them. Although we have a number of arguably more elegant sugar maples and silver maples scattered around the yard, as well as the much smaller native vine maple along with several sensational Japanese varieties, there'll always be room for bigleaf maples too, those rambunctious deciduous giants of our native forest.

Becoming a Seed Extremist

IN THE DEPTHS of dark winter, a gardener's thoughts turn naturally to seedage. Catalogues from select seed houses appear unexpectedly in the mail. "So soon?" we muse, startled that it's already time to be ordering seeds and setting our sights anew on gardening. "While the earth remaineth," Genesis reminds us, "seedtime and harvest...shall not cease." Like a seed itself, the midwinter gardener is a compressed capsule of explosive energy awaiting the moment of emergence.

There are different levels of engagement when it comes to seeds. Some growers avoid the whole business entirely, being quite content to pick up whatever plants they require at a nursery, having left the complications of germination, pricking out and potting up to people devoted to such things. Others will nonchalantly toss into their shopping carts a random selection of picture packets off the seed rack at the supermarket. More serious types will dutifully thumb through catalogues and thoughtfully order whatever seeds are essential for their purposes. For emotive seedspeople, the perusal of catalogues is an almost sensual affair, ripe with excitements and perhaps forbidden pleasures. At the very top (or bottom) of this seedy pecking order are the seed extremists, wild-eyed characters for whom all aspects of seedage—harvesting, threshing, cleaning, storing, stratification, germination—are the very stuff of life itself.

Like many a gardener, I find myself somewhere in the middle of the pack. Sandy and I grow all our vegetables from seed, along with certain perennials and a smattering of annuals. Easy things, like beans and peas, are no-brainers to save. Seeds from tomatoes and peppers take a bit more fussing, but we do those too. Certain others—'Red Russian' kale, New Zealand spinach, chervil and cilantro—we leave to self-seed. For the rest, we purchase organic seeds, but always with a niggling sense that one ought to be doing more—saving the seeds of almost everything, even dabbling in cross-pollination. Becoming, in short, a seed extremist oneself.

Perhaps the best way to assess the consequences of such a decision is to observe seed extremists in action, and that's quite readily done by attending a Seedy Saturday. A relatively recent phenomenon, these events are now hugely popular, attracting diverse crowds of seed savers and shoppers and providing better people-watching opportunities than Grand Central Station. Hence it was that when invited to participate in Victoria's annual Seedy Saturday, I made haste to attend.

Entering through the big glass doors of the Victoria Conference Centre was like stepping into a seedy version of Caesars Palace. Hundreds of people were milling about and jabbering excitedly. Scarcely through the door, I ran smack up against the Community Seed Swap, on whose tables lay hundreds of packets of seeds contributed by community members. The booth people were wheeling and dealing in seeds as smoothly as any blackjack dealer. All manner of common and exotic seeds could be had for a pittance in comparison with the inflationary prices at the big seed houses. Other booths—including Dan Jason's iconic Salt Spring Seeds, Full Circle Seeds, and Stellar Seeds—offered a wholesome diversity of locally adapted, organic and heritage seeds. Throughout the day, speakers addressed topics such as Edible Landscaping, Starting from Seed, Slow Food, and Terminator Technology.

With this many extreme seeders all crowded into one spot, you'd expect the conversations to be arcane enough to mystify a mystic, and they didn't disappoint. Elaborate discussions concerning ideal temperatures and humidity levels for seed dry-down; anticipated germination percentages; the difference between simple dormancy and double dormancy; how to bag the "king" heads of parsnips; the disappointments of "off-types"; and the pathos of self-sterile hybrids—here was seedage elevated to the level of both science and art.

And you know in your bones that what's being discussed and distributed at events like these is correct. That hulking multinational corporations now have a stranglehold on the worldwide development, production and distribution of seeds. That they've made a nasty habit of buying up smaller seed houses and extinguishing seed types not to their fancy. That these same corporate behemoths also produce and market the chemical fertilizers, herbicides, fungicides and insecticides required to bolster their skittish seedlings. That new crop varieties are developed, increasingly with genetic modification, not for their taste or nutritional value, but rather for the economic advantage of uniformity in colour, size and ripening time, along with adaptability to handling, shipping and storage.

The corporatization of seedage is resulting in a potentially catastrophic loss of genetic diversity, with untold hundreds of heirloom varieties having slipped into extinction in recent years. Options, alternatives and, ultimately, food security are compromised as the gene pool narrows into the treacherous tunnel of micropropagation and terminator technology.

Seed savers' exchanges stand as a bulwark against this genetic recklessness. And that's what is truly marvellous about a Seedy Saturday, bolstered by the number of young activists in attendance. It's not just a fun event or merely a way of acquiring the seeds of unusual and interesting varieties at bargain prices. It's also a political act of the finest sort. A bold statement of opposition to corporate pollution and draining of the gene pool, and a celebration of the precious genetic heritage embedded within a seed and released by the care and attention of devoted seedspersons.

GARDEN PLOTS

Catkin Call

LIKE A GARDENING version of the Cinderella story, there comes an intriguing interlude early in the year when certain nondescript bit players suddenly emerge as undisputed stars of the garden. The earliest flowering bulbs, the Chinese witch hazel, winter-flowering jasmine and *Viburnum × bodnantense* all have their moments of glory in the dull muddle of February slopping into March. But none can quite compare with the sight of pale late-winter sunshine illuminating a mass of golden catkins. It's a spectacle to damn near break your heart with beauty, a vision of hopefulness and fruitfulness and sassy defiance of the drear days.

At our place, that show's at its most splendid amid the contorted twigs of the hazel called Harry Lauder's walking stick, *Corylus avellana* 'Contorta'. All along its bronzed and twisted branches, pendant male catkins dangle their rows of tiny flowers made brilliant with yellow pollen. Like the shrub itself, they're viewed to wonderful effect from underneath, the catkins and serpentine limbs forming a dazzling pattern against the pale-blue late-winter sky. None of this was in our minds years ago when we planted the hazel high up in the hollow centre of an enormous western red cedar stump. But now, oh, how terribly clever! Both stump and tree were things of beauty, and never more so than at catkin time.

Looking down on catkins can be dazzling too, as I discovered one March when flying over Vancouver Island. Ever alert for the latest eco-disaster, I thought at first I was seeing countless dead trees in the forest, as though mountain pine beetles had suddenly descended upon the coast. But as we glided down into the Comox Valley, I realized that the rusty-brown quilt spread across the woods was actually the canopy of red alder trees transformed by a dusting of catkins.

"In the wind of windy March / The catkins drop down / Curly, caterpillar-like, / Curious green and brown." That's how poet Christina Rossetti saw them. And, yes, they are curious creations. My *Oxford Dictionary* defines the catkin as "a unisexual inflorescence, consisting of rows of apetalous flowers ranged in circles along a slender stalk, the whole forming a cylindrical, downy-looking, usually pendant, spike." It's also called an ament or amentum.

All manner of trees bear them—including hazel, beech and oak—and they're a favourite of the fast-growing and short-lived species like poplar, willow, alder and birch. In the hazel family, the catkins have only male flowers. Their companion female flowers are found on a higher branch— tiny but often very colourful. On the other hand, species in the willow family produce catkins that are either male or female; they are set on different plants to prevent inbreeding. Often blooming at a time of year when insects are in short supply, catkins rely upon the wind to carry their abundant pollen to the female flowers. It's an amazingly effective system, as omnipresent red alders amply testify: they can, and do, seed in at fifty thousand seedlings per hectare.

But it's their late-winter cheerfulness for which we love catkins best. And none more so, I think, than the pussy willows. For many willow species, it's the male plants that produce the finest catkins. They're called pussy willows, not to encourage schoolboy sniggering, but for the obvious reason that they're cat-like in their soft, furry silkiness.

The classic pussy willow is *Salix discolor*, whose slender reddish stems bear silky, soft pearl-grey catkins well over an inch long. In the proper hands they do, anyway. Our specimen does not. Too long crowded in by larger trees, regularly brutalized by roving gangs of deer, and, several winters back, clobbered by a gigantic toppled fir tree, it produces a paucity of pussy willows dismally strung along skeletal twigs. Cuttings of it that we've given away to friends have developed into giants by comparison. Not to be outdone, we've planted a whip in a more favourable location and have high hopes.

The French or pink pussy willow, *Salix caprea*, produces rotund, greyish-pink catkins that are also highly admired. We don't grow this one, but we do have the slightly bizarre black pussy willow, magnificently named *S. gracilistyla* 'Melanostachys'. Worth keeping around just so you make a grand impression by casually dropping its name into conversation every so often, it produces strange black catkins with brick-red anthers.

This one too we've managed to site improperly. It's so deprived of light it has taken on a peculiar horizontal posture, like someone diving straight out from the edge of a swimming pool. This brings it within easy reach of the deer and—no matter how intriguing its black and red catkins are—a stop to admire this little shrub is disconcertingly akin to visiting an ailing friend in a nursing home.

Which isn't at all what we're looking for when climbing out of the mud pit of winter. So back we scurry to the hazels, and to contorted Harry Lauder most of all, where a jubilation of golden catkins proclaims that winter's on the run and Hallelujah! spring is indeed coming in.

Chronic Underachievers

MOST GARDENS REQUIRE a touch of ruthlessness every so often, and one opportune time for stern measures is during the skinny days when late winter grudgingly gives way to early spring. Something in the briskness of air and general arousal of energies seems conducive to taking a no-nonsense approach to the place.

Easier said than done though, because by my observation gardeners generally tend more toward soft-heartedness than its opposite. Year after year, they'll tolerate chronically underperforming plants—leggy perennials that sprawl indifferently or topple beneath the slightest provocation, shrubs notorious for gangly growth but never a bloom, delinquent willows whose roots can't resist an available drainpipe, or scruffy poplars that loom over the garden like schoolyard bullies.

Oh, there's no end of miscreant plants to be found and apparently no limit to certain gardeners' willingness to tolerate them. I could give you any number of examples from our own garden, and here's just one: an emaciated berberis that has been with us for more years than I can remember. "These are cast-iron shrubs," a definitive gardening manual had advised us, implying that no adversity of climate or neglect could detract from their enduring charm. And, as in most things, there was a grain of truth to be found here, for this particular berberis proved indestructible insofar as it would never entirely expire. It might regularly shed the greater part of its foliage, leaving a sub-Saharan clump of thorns and dead twigs, but there'd always remain some small remnant patch of green, a token both of its endurance and, we imagined, of better days to come. So I'd repeatedly hesitate to tear the wretched thing up and put it out of its misery. Maybe this year it will leaf out splendidly again, I'd think, withdrawing the grub hoe just before striking a fatal blow. Sometimes a flush of new growth would indeed appear, but by midsummer, having several times backed into the thorny mass while working in the shrubbery and gotten a startling jab in the bum,

I'd be more than prepared once again to give this spiny nuisance the heave-ho.

Observers might reasonably conclude that repeated leniency toward scoundrels like this is evidence of what privileged Brits call being wet. And, yes, the notion of a plant that has underperformed for a decade or more suddenly becoming magnificent does rather smack of pathetic delusion. Preferring to put a more positive spin on things, I like to think of the gardener's reluctance to evict the poor, the weak and the huddled as having its roots in compassion laced with a bracing optimism. We want to believe that, given the right conditions, these chronic failures will pull themselves up by their botanical bootstraps and prove themselves worthy of our confidence in them. And even if they fail again, compassion bids us love them still in all their unlovableness.

Nevertheless, limits must be placed even upon loving solicitude if the garden isn't to end up a hugger-mugger of weaklings and malingerers. This was certainly the case with a rosybloom crabapple that had occupied a central position in our garden for many years. Notwithstanding a splendid rosy blossoming each spring, it was a tree of weak and sour disposition, given to numerous ailments and complaints. Invariably its purplish leaves would wither and shrivel throughout the summer, creating an unhappily cadaverous effect. In autumn it would drop countless splotchy fruits on the pathway. Its winter profile was not in any way pleasant. For years we sprayed and pruned and fussed, but mostly we grumbled, threatening eviction if things didn't improve. Then each springtime that lovely show of pink-red blossom would captivate us all over again and win the tree another year's reprieve.

Which is precisely why I propose that if there is to be ruthlessness exercised, let it be done during dormancy...before any hint of new growth starts again fashioning the illusion of a radical change for the better. This is exactly what eventually befell that tatty crabapple—branches, trunk, roots, all of it banished in the cleansing frenzy of pre-spring. And, of course, the garden is vastly the better for no longer having its haggard presence smack in the middle of things.

As for the berberis: well, that's another story, because, you know, they are cast-iron plants and you can't entirely discount the possibility that this one will finally hit its stride and leaf out brilliantly this year.

Going to the Dark Side

AT CERTAIN UNSETTLING times, a gardener may begin to suspect that her garden artistry is painting a bit too pretty a picture. That it's excessively dainty, even cloying, like the darling buds of May. It's precisely at such times that unconventional plants show their true worth. I don't mean ground-hoggers or troublesome invasives that muscle their way into a garden and then set about ruining it. Rather, plants that are a touch exotic, strange, occasionally offensive and potentially dangerous.

The voodoo lily is one of these. Nobody would ever describe her as being the prettiest thing in the garden, and certainly not as having the sweetest scent. Nevertheless, she has a peculiar allure, and an otherwise too prettified garden may be considerably enhanced by having her dark charms within it.

Before we even get to the plant itself, there's a delicious air of confusion around its botanical naming as well as its common names. Properly speaking, the genuine voodoo lily is *Sauromatum venosum,* also called *S. guttatum,* along with a baker's dozen other ringing Latin synonyms. One could almost imagine scores of semidemented taxonomists engaged in a protracted bunfight at lunch over which is the correct name. Sometimes referred to as the Indian voodoo lily, or monarch of the east, because of its Indian origins, *S. venosum* has to suffer the indignity of several near relatives each also mistakenly being referred to as a voodoo lily. The confusion includes the appellations snake palm, snake lily, cobra lily and corpse flower.

No matter what the name, the true voodoo lily comes with an unmistakable whiff of danger and of evil, involving snakes, venom and corpses. Not surprisingly, all parts of the plant are poisonous if ingested, and even handling it can cause skin irritation or other allergic reactions.

But what an intriguing piece of work it is. For years we've kept a cluster of its tubers in a five-gallon pot, which spends the winter in the greenhouse and is moved outdoors in March. By about mid-May, each tuber's furled spathe emerges from the soil and opens to reveal a greenish-white cloak speckled with purple markings (the alternative botanical name *guttatum* refers to something speckled or spotted, as if by drops). In its centre, a single deep-purple spadix stands luridly erect. Swarms of carrion flies alight upon this flower stalk (sometimes called a "jack") and its peculiar vase-like spathe. The flies are attracted to the plant by its foul odour, magnificently described by a writer for the Pacific Bulb Society: "Unlike some aroids which smell like carrion, this one emits a pervasive reek of rat feces." Within a few days, both spathe and spadix wilt miserably to the ground and the pollinating flies vanish. Shortly afterwards, a slender speckled stem surfaces and grows leaflets, so that the whole plant resembles a miniature palm tree.

But it's that initial eerie flowering stage that earns the voodoo lily her common name, conjuring images of Satanism and zombies, witch doctors, voodoo dolls and other sensationalized rubbish churned out by lowbrow authors, filmmakers and rock bands. There's an American porn actor who employs the stage name Voodoo, and at least ten different songs titled Voodoo performed by everyone from Black Sabbath to the Spice Girls. The popular perception of voodoo is a hopelessly racist muddle of myth and misconception bearing little resemblance to the clan-based Vodoun culture originally brought from West Africa to Haiti and the United States through the slave trade.

The same might be said of the misnamed voodoo lily. The ominous-sounding name *Sauromatum venosum* does not refer to the snake-like appearance of its leaf-bearing stem, nor to the cadaverous behaviour of its malodorous flower. I stumbled upon what I take to be the genuine derivation in a paper titled *Ethnobotanical Observation on Tuberous Plants from Tribal Area of Rajasthan*, written by two Indian ethnobotanists. One of their observations was that the tuber of *S. venosum* contains antidotal properties and that traditionally a paste made from it is applied to the affected area of a person who's been bitten by a snake.

I wonder if there isn't a taxonomically clever double meaning involved: that the plant is itself poisonous but also capable of drawing out the venom of a snake. However you parse it, the voodoo lily—or should I say, more fittingly, monarch of the east?—provides a provocative antidote to the excessively prettified garden.

Plant Faunaticism

THE UNFOLDINGS OF favourite plants throughout the seasons might be cause for unalloyed joy were we not so persistently confronted with animal imagery crawling, hopping, slithering and bounding around our gardens. Really, for people who should know better, it's as though we can't keep our flora and our fauna in their proper places. The trouble starts early on with skunk cabbages, those odoriferous harbingers of spring so fatally linked to a mammal with a foul anal gland. Pussy willows are far more cuddly, but already you can see a nasty trend developing. We may be momentarily distracted by the splendour of crabapples and dogwoods in full bloom, though a moment's calm reflection has us wondering whether either of these worthy trees has a bona fide association with dogs or crabs.

Catmint's legitimacy is less in doubt, since it does attract actual cats, and duckweed ducks under the bar too, on the grounds that it and ducks frequently cohabit ponds. In a pinch, the same argument might be extended to frog's-bit, and butterflies certainly do have a thing for butterfly bushes, but frankly the whole concept of a foxglove is absurd. Wouldn't logic decree that there also be a foxhat or a foxshoe?

But logic plays no part in this unseemly business of sticking animal names onto unsuspecting plants. Well, okay, maybe hedgehog holly passes muster on the basis of prickliness, and in a good mood you might be persuaded to grant the same dispensation to the monkey puzzle tree, but who in their right mind would consider that *Acanthus spinosus* could credibly be called spiny bear's breeches? I've studied these doughty perennials at length in our garden, but I'm damned if I can figure out what a spiny bear is, or how it gets into or out of breeches. Or is it the breeches that are spiny? This kind of zany naming is enough to make the pigsqueak squeak.

Same thing with snapdragons. Are dragons actually snapping, and if so, at what? Are larkspurs really spurring larks, or just trying to outmanoeuvre some threatening hawkweed? Does anyone really believe that robins awaken because of the trillium wake-robin? Please, somebody, call out for a cuckoo flower, quick! Snakes naturally slither into this problematic approach to wildlife gardening too. Thus we have snakeroot underfoot, and a snake bush, a snake-bark maple and a snake's head fritillary. The *Echium* called viper's bugloss undoubtedly refers to some tragic loss of bugs, but the meaning's lost on me.

Ah, yes, I can hear one of our dotty nomenclators protesting, "But what about zebra grass, eh?" And you have to concede the point: with the right drugs in your system, this striped *Miscanthus* does, in fact, bear a faint resemblance to a zebra. Nevertheless, you can quickly regain the upper hand by mentioning toad lily or toadflax and watch the old duffer squirm while trying to make any coherent connection between these plants and toads. If he attempts to claw his way back to credibility with a tiger lily, finish him off with a deft reference to wormwood.

As if it weren't enough of a trial having these eccentrics attempting to justify their faunaticism, chronic offenders go a step further by also involving animal body parts in the business. Lamb's ears and bunny ears and cat's ears are cute enough to pass muster, I suppose, although elephant's ears are stretching things a bit. Personally, I find cowslips and oxlip primulas unpleasantly evocative of thick-lipped bovines belching greenhouse gases.

I imagine cock's combs are reasonably harmless in their silly self-aggrandizement, still I doubt any of us would be the poorer for not having variegated cock's foot in our gardens. Parrots are all well and good in the tropics, but please spare us all these gaudy parrot's beaks and feathers. Goat's beard could definitely do with a shave, while great hound's tongue is nothing but a slobbery mess.

What can you say about staghorn ferns and staghorn sumac? To begin with, stags generally prefer to grow antlers rather than horns. Moreover, a favourite pastime of any stag of my acquaintance is to rub its velvet antlers against the trunks of our prized saplings, thereby debarking and eventually killing them. Who needs stags or their horns?

Less destructive, but scarcely more appealing, are all the plants named after the tails of creatures. You've got your burro's tail and cattails, your donkey tail sedum, lizard's tail, your foxtail lily, squirrel tail grass, rat tail cactus and all the rest. I'd be just as happy if they all turned tail and got the hell out of the garden.

Which brings us, mercifully, to the final category in this misplaced mania for animal rights among plants: namely, the banes. Bugbane to keep the bugs off, and fleabane to do the same for fleas. Wolfsbane should hold the wolves at bay, though whether we really require leopard's bane in this part of the world I leave for you to decide.

Meanwhile, I'm going out to the garden to make sure the spiderworts aren't spinning webs around the bee balm.

All these photos of Sandy and Des Kennedy's garden on Denman Island were taken by Des during 2013.

An 'Alchemist' rose and summer-flowering clematis drape from a rustic cedar arbour
above herbaceous peonies and bellflowers.

ABOVE: A bank of clipped evergreens slopes down towards the patio pool, with the rose-draped and sod-roofed woodshed beyond.

RIGHT: The polished leaves of water lilies help discourage algae growth in the pool.

OPPOSITE TOP: The massed tiny bells of salal, *Gaultheria shallon,* provide a springtime feast for nectar feeders.

OPPOSITE BOTTOM: The stately spires of foxtail lilies, *Eremurus robustus,* rise behind a sculpture of local granite, titled "Spirit of the Garden" and presented to Sandy on her fiftieth birthday by artist Michael Dennis.

So happy together: an extended family of sempervivums (TOP) squeeze
accommodatingly into a pot, while a cabal of 'Charmant' summer cabbages
(OPPOSITE BOTTOM) explore their own group dynamics.

TOP: The sumptuous blooms of tree peonies float above the dainty flowers of London pride, *Saxifraga × urbium*, along the sandstone front path.

OPPOSITE BOTTOM: The dangling catkins and contorted branches of the hazel Harry Lauder's walking stick, *Corylus avellana* 'Contorta', create an early-spring delight.

The house of hand-hewn and salvaged materials is shaded by the feathery foliage of *Gleditsia triacanthos* 'Skyline', while a summer-flowering dogwood, *Cornus kousa*, blooms as a garden star.

ABOVE: The creamy stamens and carmine petals of the Japanese peony 'Sword Dance' provide a thrilling accent point between boxwood and sandstone.

LEFT: Standing stones peer across pots of flowering sempervivum towards the indolence-inducing sunroom.

OPPOSITE TOP: Thrift-shop bling enlivens a patio chandelier of contorted hazel twigs.

OPPOSITE BOTTOM: The sun-loving foliage of golden hops, *Humulus lupulus* 'Aureus', contrasts handsomely with the purple leaves of *Ligularia dentata* 'Desdemona'.

ABOVE: Massed antique roses and honeysuckles, underplanted with geraniums, create a sweetly-perfumed prospect overlooking the hillside garden.

OPPOSITE TOP: The blooms of the English rose 'Gertrude Jekyll' are more elegant, but the humble flowers of dame's rocket, *Hesperis matronalis,* are highly scented and provide a preferred nectar for butterflies.

OPPOSITE BOTTOM: Under of the gentle gaze of "Mataji," carved from salvaged red cedar by artist Richard Menard, a sandstone alcove curves towards a weeping Japanese maple beneath which a small stream cascades into the patio pool.

TOP: Perfectly serviceable old hand tools are hijacked in the name of art
to gussy up a shed wall.

TOP: An old cedar stump provides a rustic pedestal and frame
for reddish flights of fancy.

BOTTOM: Near the forest's edge, leaves of giant butterbur, *Petasites japonicus*,
congregate across the enormous trunk of a fallen Douglas fir.

TOP: The flawlessly white bracts of *Cornus kousa* will give way to strawberry-like fruits that are a favourite food of many birds.

BOTTOM: White fireweed, *Epilobium angustifolium* f. *album,* provides a brilliant backdrop for pink roses.

TOP: Rambunctious plumes of goat's beard, *Aruncus dioicus*, are mirrored farther up the hill by the floating cloud of tiny flowers produced by the greater sea kale, *Crambe cordifolia*.

BOTTOM: Exuberant 'Purple Sensation' ornamental onions mingle with tree peony blooms in a springtime celebration.

Mounds of clipped Korean box, *Buxus microphylla* var. *koreana,* undulate around a bronze fennel, *Foeniculum vulgare* 'Purpureum', and a clematis 'Niobe' towards the covered patio and hillside beyond.

Midsummer Dreamin'

THE ALL-SEASON GARDEN is much the rage these days, especially on the West Coast where it's possible, even arguably desirable, to produce a brilliant succession of "shows" throughout the year. Late blooms on last season's roses, hydrangeas and 'Autumn Joy' sedum segue almost seamlessly into the midwinter delights of the pale-pink flowers of 'Christmas Cheer' rhododendron and the clustered waxy white blooms of the Christmas rose.

There's a robust egalitarianism in all of this, a levelling of the horticultural playing field, as though all plants, regardless of seasonal preference, were beneficiaries of a federally funded equal-opportunity program. A February bloom's no less delightsome than is one in June. I'm all for it, so long as this equipollency doesn't obscure the obvious: that a garden may, perhaps even should, achieve for a certain limited time an absolute apotheosis, a dizzying pinnacle from whose heights the remainder of the year, for all its charms, appears as mere prelude on the one side and denouement on the other.

For many coastal growers, that moment of unrivalled glory occurs each spring when the rhodos and azaleas, the dogwoods and crabapples, spring bulbs and all the rest, achieve an acme of perfection. At our place, midsummer is the moment. Somewhere right around summer solstice, the garden takes a spectacular leap out of the ordinary into the realms of pure rapture. For one thing, the antique roses are mostly blooming now, dozens of bushes smothered in voluptuous blooms of pale pink, pure white, deep maroon. Their ethereal perfumes waft across the gardens and mingle with other lovely fragrances—the heady scent of dame's rocket, *Hesperis matronalis,* the cinnamon spicy musk of dianthus, the citrus-like essence of mock orange, and the voluptuous perfume of honeysuckle, which American garden-writer Celia Thaxter described as "like the spirit of romance, sweet as youth's tender dreams. It is summer's very soul."

Visual delights almost rival the inebriating scents. Delphiniums stand as stately spires in blues and whites and dreamy lavenders. The flaming silken petals of poppies run riot across the hillside as though it were a Monet canvas. Fulsome heads of herbaceous peonies form mesmerizing swirls of petals. The Jerusalem sage, *Phlomis fruticosa,* has erected its peculiar tiers of bold sulphur-yellow flower clusters. Ornamental alliums explode into tiny astral galaxies of bloom. The great Arabian thistle, *Onopordum arabicum,* bristles with brilliant silver-grey foliage. Summer-flowering clematis vines pour cascades of mauve and blue and white blooms down their obelisks.

For a few incomparable weeks, all of nature seems to conspire in this midsummer dream. The longest days of the year open with birdsong mornings of shining golden-green and end with glowing, warmly scented evenings. The first fawns of the year come tiptoeing out of the woods, impossibly lovable despite all the damage they'll wreak later on. The violet-green swallows fledge in a splendid burst of aerial acrobatics. Rufous hummingbirds careen recklessly around the garden, flitting from honeysuckle trumpets to the Peruvian lilies. Big swallowtail butterflies drift like floating petals, alighting on delphiniums and dianthus to sip their sweet nectar. The whole garden hums like rush hour with the business of nectar-mad bees.

Yes, we swoon, but all too soon we drop a notch again. The summer drought begins to bite. Aphids multiply exponentially. The hummingbirds desert us for who knows where, perhaps wildflower meadows on the mountains. The swallowtails turn tail too. The garden's still rich with treasures, of course. The lilies come on with their own divine night fragrances, and nicotiana and evening-scented stocks. Hydrangeas flaunt their outrageous excesses. No, there's plenty of pleasure still to be had in the months ahead. But never quite that same over-the-top exhilaration we experience at midsummer—that glorious combination of freshness, warmth, scent and colour, and the explosion of birds and insects, when the sun is at its highest in the sky.

Prudent souls might argue we'd be better served by holding a steadier course, avoiding the excitements of exhilaration so as to be spared their counterbalancing times of gloom. Not me. I wouldn't trade those few ecstatic weeks of walking through the gardens of the gods for all the equanimity in the Buddha's bowl. Perhaps great gardeners can maintain this kind of peak performance throughout the year, though you'd think the old heart would expire from the explosive excitement of it all. For myself, as dedicated as the next zealot to an all-season garden, and inclined to become excitable over the various charms of the seasons, I nevertheless especially cherish those few brief weeks at the apex of the year when one gets to partake of the truly divine.

Moon Trance

IT'S DURING THE great festivities around summer solstice that midsummer madness is said to be at its height. Now's the season when the light of the midsummer moon supposedly inspires a particularly elevated form of lunacy. We might easily apply these ancient notions to the contemporary antics of various celebrities and headmen—not to mention the lamentable attempts at "Midnight Madness" promoted by insalubrious shopping malls—but I prefer the sweeter lunacy of gardening.

A garden is definitely one fine place to be on Midsummer Night, although a woodland glade has much to offer too. This is the very night upon which Oberon, King of the Faeries, gathers the magical seeds of ferns from which he derives his invisibility. Long before *Lord of the Rings,* an old Danish tradition had it that anyone positioned under an elder bush at midnight on Midsummer Night will see the King of Faeryland and all his retinue pass by.

This is precisely what I propose to do on solstice night, and for good measure we have not one, but three types of elders growing at our place. The red elder, *Sambucus racemosa,* blooms in early spring with panicles of small creamy-white flowers, followed by clusters of red berries that ripen in July. These fetch in robins and wood pigeons that methodically strip the bushes of ripe fruit. Similar in appearance, the blue elder, *S. caerulea,* blooms and fruits later, its disc-like clusters of small flowers being particularly attractive to bees and butterflies. The clusters of blue berries that follow lure the wood pigeons back, along with big flickers that dance among the branches and gobble the fruit.

These two elders are natives, but very similar to the European elder, *S. nigra,* which has long been revered as a mystic plant capable of curing all sorts of ills—I once relied upon a tincture of it for removing warts—as well as providing a location for faery sightings. I have fond memories of this bush from my days as a little chap in England gathering bags of berries for my mum to make her elderberry wine. We now have two developed forms of *nigra* growing in the garden: 'Black Beauty' has deep-purple foliage, and the stunning 'Black Lace' displays finely cut and intensely purple-black leaves. Both bear large, flat heads of small pinkish-purple flowers followed by purple-black berries. 'Black Lace' especially has been very much in vogue in recent years, hailed as being "different" and "unusual," while also being extremely easy to grow.

But back to faeryism. I realize the risks one runs in even raising the topic, especially with a New Age–provoked fascination with faeries having run rampant through the marketplace in recent years. Nevertheless, belief in these tiny, sometimes mischievous, spirits lingers through the folklore and literature of many cultures. No less an authority than J.R.R. Tolkien warned that "Faerie is a perilous land, and in it are pitfalls for the unwary and dungeons for the overbold." Thackeray was cautious too: "Fairy roses, fairy rings, turn out sometimes troublesome things."

From whatever perspective they're viewed, faeries are invariably associated with flowers—"Garden faeries come at dawn," "all the fairy train / For pinks and daisies search'd the flow'ry plain," "Each fairy breath of summer, as it blows with loveliness, inspires the blushing rose," and on and on. So it stands to reason that all sorts of plants, typically small flowers of meadows, woodlands and mountains, are named for the little people. The faery primrose is the old cowslip primrose, *Primula veris,* which blooms wild in fields in Britain and Europe, and now graces many a spring garden like our own. The faery foxglove, *Erinus,* is a little tufted perennial bearing racemes of small purple flowers native to the mountains of central Europe. Another mountain dweller, the faery lantern, *Calochortus,* thrives in the Sierra and Rocky Mountains of the West. Small tulip-like plants that grow from corms, they tend to be short-lived in gardens and far happier in their mountain haunts.

Gracefulness distinguishes the faery flowers. The faery wand or angel's fishing rod, *Dierama pulcherrimum,* is native to South Africa, with sword-like leaves and tall, slender arching stems that dangle pendulous bell-shaped flowers of mauve, purple or white. It's especially fine hanging over a pool, and I saw it used to grand effect in Helen Dillon's Dublin garden, where she had combined it with similar-coloured flowers of perennial sweet pea. Faery grass, *Briza media,* is an annual quaking grass, native to the Mediterranean area, bearing graceful nodding bronze-coloured fruit clusters. Faery flax, *Linum catharticum,* is noted for its delicate texture and small flowers. And faery bells, *Disporum,* is a genus of flowering perennials best suited to moist woodland gardens, which produces clusters of dangling bell-shaped greenish-white flowers in spring.

Tolkien and Thackeray notwithstanding, Faeryland, the imagined realm of faeries, is a place, like these plants, of charm and delicate beauty. Its signature properties—enchantment, magic and sweet illusion—are also at the heart of every fine garden. At the risk of being hauled away by some psychological SWAT team and held in a padded cell for my own good, I'll venture the opinion that a gardener's highest calling is to create an environment in which faeries, nymphs, sylphs, dryads and other of the little people might easily be at home. Meanwhile, I'll be taking up my post beside an elder bush by the light of the lunatic midsummer moon.

Ivy Beleaguered

ON FIRST MENTION, an "ivy pull" might be mistaken for some esoteric form of tug-o-war involving teams of Morris dancers at a suburban medieval faire. But it's no such thing. A contemporary ivy pull is serious business, involving lethal force, penance for past transgressions and a certain evangelical zeal. Its objective is straightforward enough: the eradication of invasive ivy from locations where it does not belong and is not desired. But the metaphysics of the thing are as deep as ivy roots themselves and as tortuous as the vine's twisted growth patterns.

To begin with, English ivy is no featherweight in the botanical ring. A member of the ginseng family, from its origins in the Caucasus Mountains it spread through western Asia and Europe, becoming in the Greco-Roman world sacred to the wine god Dionysus (Bacchus), a deity not to be taken lightly. In one classical legend, he created ivy from the corpse of the nymph Cissos, who danced with such joyful abandon she fell dead at his feet from exhaustion. This mythological precursor of the all-inclusive beachfront holiday eventually led to the tradition of ivy wreaths hanging above the doorways of taverns and wine shops, and to certain conflicted Romans wearing ivy garlands in the hopes of staving off drunkenness during the bacchanals. For the Druids, the plant symbolized the feminine principle, something also not to be taken lightly. The vine was purposively brought to North America by colonists and widely planted to quickly cover "waste ground," especially banks, and for its ability to suppress weeds and thrive in shade.

This history—the colonial bit, not the bacchanalian—pretty well mirrors our own experience. When we started out in a dusty and desolate patch of logged-over ground, the one plant that would grow quickly and uncomplainingly was English ivy. That should have been a tipoff, but we were young, and desperate for any small sign that we were making headway in the slow business of transforming a tangle of logging slash into a homestead. So ivy got its roots in about the same time we did.

Its attributes are not inconsiderable. It's easy to propagate, grows vigorously in full sun or deep shade, is drought tolerant once established and can be pruned or sheared to shape. Its adaptability for horizontal or vertical landscaping derives from the adventitious rootlets that form along the stems, allowing the vine to root as a dense ground cover or to climb high, clinging to walls, trees or other vertical surfaces. English ivy has an entrenched reputation for destroying brick walls, but some authorities maintain the opposite, that against sound walls it promotes dryness and warmth, reduces weathering and adds beauty. Draped curtains of ivy are a fine way to disguise the sullen blankness of a cement-block wall or the imprisoning effects of a chain-link fence. Rubble piles and other blots on the landscapes can be converted into pleasing green mounds, and old stumps or snags turned into attractive leafy towers when festooned with ivy. The dense foliage of mature vines makes ideal nesting sites for many bird species, especially those needing a snug home before deciduous trees are fully leafed out. Hummingbirds, cardinals, towhees and song sparrows all nest in it.

In this optimistic spirit, we ran ivy up a derelict power pole, turning what had been an eyesore into a greeny spire frequented by songbirds. We planted it alongside the pumphouse, an unfortunate little structure that resembled a disgraced outhouse. Ivy quickly transformed it into a leafy hummock whose extra layers assisted in preventing winter freeze-up of the waterworks. In early winter these "arborescent" ivies (as opposed to the perpetually juvenile form crawling on the ground) would break into flower, casting a yeasty perfume that would attract wild bees and other nectar feeders. In midwinter, hungry deer (typically indifferent to the "deer-proof plants" list) would strip whatever leaves they could reach. In short, the ivy seemed an altogether positive addition to the landscape. Nor were we alone in our enthusiasm. Certain public show gardens feature topiaries in which ivy cultivars like 'Midget', 'Misty', 'Pixie' and 'Golden Ingot' are clipped to the shapes of unicorns, faeries, gnomes and the like. No doubt about it, the right ivy in the right place and the right hands can make a worthy contribution to the garden.

Why then these bullish ivy pullers? Because certain types of what we call English ivy, however benign they might be in other locales, become a menace in the mild, moist climes of the Pacific Northwest. Here they threaten ecosystems and impoverish biodiversity by smothering and shading native grasses, mosses and wildflowers, and even shrubs and trees, eliminating habitat and food for birds, animals and insects. Amazingly, even sizable Douglas fir trees can be choked to death by this aggressor. In some forested areas of Oregon and Washington, dense carpets of ivy have created "ivy deserts" of degraded biodiversity. Both states have placed certain types of ivy on their Noxious Weed List.

It's critical, however, that we not succumb to ivy hysteria. Out of some four hundred English ivy cultivars, only four have been identified as invasive in the Pacific Northwest: *Hedera helix* 'Baltica', 'California', 'Pittsburgh' and 'Star', along with *Hedera hibernica,* known as Atlantic or Irish ivy but sometimes sold as English ivy. But that gang of five has caused enough trouble to give ivy a very bad name and provoked a vigorous push-back. In Vancouver's Stanley Park, where ivy stands accused of having a significant negative impact on the diversity and composition of native vegetation, regularly scheduled ivy pulls draw hundreds of robust volunteers—aptly dubbed "Ivy Busters"—who are systematically yanking out the dark invader.

Against this epic backdrop, in due course I too became a born-again ivy puller. But the name's a tad misleading, implying that one simply takes a firm hold, pulls vigorously, and out pops the offending plant. The reality, at least in our stony ground, was that an ivy pull more typically entailed a pitched battle of furious bloodthirstiness. "My Great Pumphouse War" was a classic of the genre. The ivy had over the years pushed its way through cedar shakes covering the walls and roof, penetrated the sheathing beneath and set up a vast network of arterial stems inside the walls. Its roots had burrowed under the building and were well on their way toward Earth's molten core. I attacked with a battery of weapons—loppers, chainsaw, grub-hoe, pickaxe and pry bar. The ivy fought back with vast reserves of stubborn spitefulness. Profanity fouled the air. After almost a week of hand-to-vine combat, I'd eliminated all trace of the monster above and below ground.

Throughout the following months we kept careful watch for new shoots, convinced that the ivy would reappear and that the battle would need to be rejoined. We had come to think of ivy, much like Scottish broom, as a perfidious antagonist from which we would never be free. But the pumphouse ivy, along with several other big clusters of invasive varieties, was gone, eliminated more readily than paranoia in gullible humans.

Our ivy-pulling careers at a close, we now can take untroubled delight in a number of more civilized variegated ivies in the garden—none of which, thus far at least, have been clipped into pixies or faeries, and none, I trust, that will ever push me into a pull.

Smell Bent

A FEW YEARS back, the fashion magazines were all atwitter about new "designer fragrances" with peculiar scents evocative of dirt, gasoline and the interior of new automobiles. All terribly cutting edge in its own way, one supposes. But, in reality, when it comes to peculiar perfumes, the merchants of scent trail hopelessly behind the gardener.

Any arborescent English ivy that escapes the notice of devoted ivy pullers will produce an unmistakable perfume from its peculiar little club-like flowers. Provocative and pungent, there is something yeasty and fermentative in the aroma, redolent of rising bread or bean curds in a tofu shop. It's an eccentric scent, quirky and a bit disconcerting, slightly salacious in some indefinable way, and all the more evocative for being cast during the darkening days of approaching winter.

Part of the collateral damage from our great pumphouse war was loosing the annual experience of that bracing yeasty scent, and I regret its loss, but something rather close to it is the fragrance cast by the Spanish chestnut, *Castanea sativa*. I remember first getting a whiff of it while staying in an old residential section of Vancouver's east side. The whole neighbourhood was suffused with a musky smell of such allure that Sandy and I set off to track down its source. Eventually, in an old churchyard, we came upon several very large trees blooming with spiky catkins of small creamy-yellow flowers from which the intriguing scent was wafting. We decided on the spot that we must have one of these big chestnuts, and now we do. This is the tree whose sweet nuts are traditionally found roasting by an open fire. A Mediterranean native, but hardy to zone five, you'd perhaps wonder why it isn't planted more widely, or at least as frequently as the somewhat coarser horse chestnut. The reason? Apparently a prudish distaste for its suggestive scent. Yes, one of our manuals warns: "Size, litter and disagreeable odour of pollen make it a tree for wide-open spaces."

And here we run smack into the sniffy issue of subjectivity concerning scents. What the great British rosarian Graham Stuart Thomas called "the diverse aromas of plants" can trigger an equal diversity of responses in people. What's desirable to one may be disagreeable to the next. The sweet scents of roses, honeysuckle and lilies may have an almost universal appeal, but the attractiveness of heady or pungent odours very much depends upon the nose of the beholder.

The lowly skunk cabbage (I prefer the name swamp lantern myself) is another fine plant unduly maligned because of its edgy odour. Blooming brilliantly in late-winter marshes and wetlands, it's a flower lush and lovely enough for the tropics but denigrated due to its scent and derogatory common name. Even expert noses sniff it differently. "All parts of the plant give a strong skunk-like odour, but only when bruised," says one. "Nearly all of its mephitic odour is confined to its roots and enormous leaves," says another. A third claims: "The skunk cabbages are slandered in their name: their flowers and leaves are not in the least skunky. But they are redolent of fermenting cabbage." Plainly no consensus among those noses.

The maidenhair tree, *Ginkgo biloba*, is another specimen with scent issues. These are among the most ancient of all trees, dating back more than two hundred million years. Once widespread, then driven almost to extinction, they are now frequently planted in urban areas because of their resistance to noxious fumes. (Just why certain urbanites will tolerate a toxic stew of hydrocarbon and other lethal fumes more readily than the scent of a sweet chestnut bloom is a matter for another discussion.) We have a couple of young ginkgos growing at our place, both of them male. Females are not planted because of their reputedly "messy and foul-smelling fruits." I've never had a whiff of them myself, so have no way of knowing if this banishment was provoked by the same prim nostrils that find the swamp lantern and Spanish chestnut malodorous.

By early summer, the odd-aromas department is occupied by valerian, *Valeriana officinalis*. "The scent is a little musty, but is obviously evocative," writes Ontario gardening-author Patrick Lima. Others have muttered that it's evocative of dirty socks. The roots of this tall herb were used traditionally to concoct a sleep-inducing sedative, and it's said that even smelling its strong odour in the garden can bring on a languid drowsiness. Being increasingly prone to the insomnia of aging, I personally quite like this soporific redolence and we keep a clump of valerian growing near the front gate.

Geraniums (not the misnamed pelargoniums) also have a curious but pleasing aroma, particularly after rain or when the plants are stepped on. We have great swathes of several varieties, grown for both their beauty and their ability to suppress weeds. An added bonus is that their strange smell, because it emanates from the leaves rather than the flowers, can be encountered at all times of the year.

I'm intrigued by our responses to these offbeat fragrances. Words fail us, as they invariably do whenever the talk turns to describing scents and their subliminal effects. Certainly memory is a part of it, and emotion and imagination, in a swirl of sensations we can't quite identify. Obviously, we would not want to be denied the attar of roses or the clove perfume of dianthus. But neither would I be denied the yeasty, musky and pungent scents of these more peculiar performers.

The Ins of Outlaws

THE MOST APPEALING gardens, it seems to me, invariably have a few disreputable plants skulking in the corners. While the primness of primulas and fussiness of fritillarias are all well and good in their own way, a garden may suffer if it is entirely given over to conformity and control. A rebel or two may be required for biodiversity's sake, an outlaw element of plants more notable for roguishness than rectitude.

We have a number of these on our grounds, one of the most dramatic being the Japanese butterbur, *Petasites japonicus* var. *giganteus,* alias bog rhubarb or giant butterbur. Sometimes referred to as a "monster textural plant," it's the most robust of the many butterburs that thrive in the north temperate regions of Europe and Asia. In its native Japan, it's called fuki. A knot of it has colonized an inhospitable corner of our yard where the soil is impossible and the shade quite dense for much of the day. It's one of the conveniences of outlaws that they'll bed down in rough conditions without complaint.

Around that point in late winter when any sign of growth seems a heaven-sent miracle, several dozen primeval-looking scapes emerge from the cold earth, quickly becoming crowned with dense corymbs of small yellowish-white, daisy-like flowers. I studied them closely this past March and was intrigued to see the flowers were swarming with tiny black flies whose slender wings glinted coppery in the thin late-winter sunshine. Shortly after, robust leaf stalks (petioles) surge from the earth, purplish with white ribbing, each eventually bearing a single kidney-shaped leaf up to a metre in diameter. Chest-high and shiny green at the outset, the lightly toothed leaves have a remarkable texture, like kid leather. As though to keep up with the surge of the stalks, the scapes also elongate after bloom. In the warm breezes of spring, the great leaves flutter like the attentive ears of green elephants.

As the season progresses, the leaves become mottled with rusty red. Some years, banana slugs rasp large holes in the leaves, other years not.

Evolved for capturing sparse sunlight in shady conditions, the big leaves wilt when exposed to blazing summer sun, but revivify with the return of shade. In autumn the tattered leaves are smudged with surreal smears of rusts and yellows, and finish the season sprawled dramatically on the ground. From emergence to decline, there's a prehistoric ambience around these plants, similar to that of gunnera, evoking ancient jungles and the banks of misty wild waterways. In their native Japan and Korea petasites was traditionally cultivated as a vegetable. The spring growth, particularly high in vitamin C, was used in a variety of dishes, but only after rigorous preparatory treatments to reduce the plant's toxicity and astringency. Introduced to the West Coast by Japanese immigrants, petasites still retain the attributes of wildness.

Some authorities warn against their cultivation because of invasiveness. Their method of expansion is not by seeding, but rather by the spread of thick, creeping underground rhizomes. However, like space and time, invasiveness is subject to great relativity. There's no question that in ideal conditions—rich soil with a constant supply of moisture—these bog rhubarbs would quickly become an uncontrollable menace, like the wild gunnera patches bedevilling farmers in the west of Ireland. But take away the moisture and good soil, and the monsters can be brought to heel. In our hardscrabble patch they've expanded only marginally over the course of several decades.

But here's a shrewd bit of irony these large-leafed rogues have worked on us: they share the ground on the edge of our woods with that bane of so many gardeners, common horsetail, *Equisetum arvense*. Both are tenacious and rhizomatous, with ineradicable rhizomes running deep in the earth. Both produce two separate stems, but rather than a flowering scape followed by leaves, horsetail first puts up a fertile stem tipped with a spore-producing cone, and then later a vegetative stem resembling a miniature pine tree with plume-like branches. Some species of petasites are commonly called sweet coltsfoot, so we've got a clever little horsey parallel involved as well.

The butterbur remains huddled in its semishaded corner, statuesque but without expansive tendencies, while the sun-loving horsetail is forever reaching out across the lawns toward our flower beds. From a gardening perspective, the horsetail represents by far the greater menace. Gardeners afflicted by invasive horsetail typically spend several years in woebegone weeding, followed by a painful period of defeatism and eventual catatonia. And so these twin troublemakers present us with a clever dilemma, involving the fine distinctions to be drawn between alien and invasive. The petasites is an introduced alien that may become hugely invasive in favourable conditions. The horsetail is a native, and not invasive in the sense of disrupting an ecosystem, but maddeningly invasive in any garden whose walls it manages to breach.

The moral of the story being that a few disreputable sorts may add a certain piquancy to the garden, but you want to be very selective about which rogue is in vogue, as there's a definite limit to how much roguish-ness any gardener may be expected to tolerate.

Ghostly Gardening

TO TRULY APPRECIATE the soulfulness of All Hallows Eve, it's advisable to slip away from the costume party for a moment and step outdoors to take a turn around the darkened garden, for in its shadowy depths the ersatz ghosts and goblins tipsily flirting indoors give way to deeper and more ancient mysteries.

Certain of the spectral evergreens, for example, have traditionally been associated with death and burial—one, *Juniperus recurva*, is even called the coffin juniper because its resinous wood was reputedly used in the making of coffins, although I prefer another of its common names, Himalayan weeping juniper. Similarly resistant to decay, cypress wood was used in fashioning mummy cases for Egyptian aristocrats and coffins for distinguished Greeks. So, for millennia, cypresses have symbolized the soul's descent into the darkness; that's why so many were planted around old cemeteries and at the head of graves. These are the trees of the dark forces of the netherworld, the Furies and Fates. The same holds true for yew trees, and in many an ancient Irish graveyard we saw large yews still growing amid listing gravestones alongside the ruins of churches. The Irish poet Thomas Rolleston described such sites a century ago: "Darkly grows the quiet ivy, / pale the broken arches glimmer through; / Dark upon the cloister-garden / dreams the shadow of the ancient yew."

In the old Celtic calendar, the last night of October was "old year's night," the night of all the witches, and particularly at this time of year no good garden should be devoid of bewitchment. A weed to some, a lovely native grass to others, witchgrass or old witchgrass, *Panicum capillare*, is a tuft-forming annual grass native to eastern North America. It has broad leaves and stems that rise a metre tall, each bearing a dense panicle of tiny greenish spikelets on delicate stalks. For real witchery, you can't do better than the common mullein, *Verbascum thapsus*, known as witch's candle or hag's taper. In pre-Christian Europe, its thick flowering stalks were dipped in tallow, set alight and carried in ritual processions (something the Halloween gang back in the house would likely join enthusiastically, if alerted). From these fecund beginnings, the mullein gained a reputation as a potent charm against demons and malignant spirits, and it's for this reason we always have a few growing at our place. Although more recently developed varieties such as 'Gainsborough' flower more profusely and tower more majestically, they have not been conclusively shown to repel malignant spirits as reliably as old witch's candle.

Neither, for that matter, has devil's club, *Oplopanax horridus,* but this infernally spiny shrub can repel just about anything else, including roaming dogs, delinquent juveniles or even heavily armed intruders. It grows wild on the West Coast, typically in moist woodlands where it forms an impenetrable and tropical-looking understorey. Its sparse and spiny branches twist up about two metres high, bearing few but large leaves. In late summer, it produces umbels of small greenish-white flowers followed by clusters of red berries that are known to attract bears. Brush against this prickly customer, and you'll get scratched by spines that emit a poison that inflames the scratches. In other words, devil's club is precisely the type of plant no reasonable gardener would cultivate, but it doesn't take much of a search to find enthusiasts growing it in their native-plant woodland gardens.

Ghostliness can haunt a garden every bit as much as devilishness and witchery. The ghost plant, *Artemisia lactiflora,* is a hardy perennial from China that shows splendidly in late summer. Around August, it produces flowering stalks about two metres tall that bear creamy plumes of ivory-tinged flowers that work handsomely as a foil to stronger colours such as bold reds or gleaming yellows. For many years, we had several of these ghost plants growing among thalictrums of matching height, whose ethereal clusters of powdery-blue flowers mingled artfully with the ivory artemisia blooms. Eventually, the ghost plant left us—as ghosts often do—mostly because she demanded more regular soaking than we were willing to provide.

Perhaps my favourite ghost of all is *Eryngium giganteum,* known as Miss Willmott's Ghost, after the great British plantswoman Ellen Willmott. A large biennial eryngium, it has a striking silvery presence, especially by moonlight or as dusk descends. Its central stalk of metallic blue-grey branches into multiple flowering shoots, and at the tip of each sits a flower head of stiff and finely pointed bracts etched in silvery white. At their centre is a cone sheathed in tiny flowers that, when their nectar's flowing, attract swarms of feeding bees. Silvery-green at first, the cones gradually turn blue grey. Somewhat invasive if not kept in check, this is a ghostly garden presence that only decency prevents me from describing as "to die for."

We could go on and on about spectral plants—into the greenhouse where the bizarre voodoo lily emerges in spring (but then I've already delved into her particular allures so won't repeat myself) or where could be discovered the secretive datura, also of voodoo legend. We might examine the peculiar little bushy cactus called dancing bones or the euphorbia known as Gorgon's head. But, enough. Time to straighten up our ridiculous costume and slip quietly back into the party, away from the mysteries found in the darkened garden of All Hallows Eve.

AVANT-GARDENERS

Stumpage Spree

AMONG THE MORE subtle joys of gardening is the great delight to be taken over particular chronicles that may extend across a garden for decades. Veteran gardeners might rejoice all the more at the sight of a prized magnolia in full bloom because they remember the scrawny little whip it was when they planted it on a chilly afternoon all those years ago, and how they nursed it and coddled it and defended it from depredation. I derive a similar, and perhaps idiosyncratic, pleasure from the big cedar stumps scattered around our garden, for they too have an extended tale to tell of youth and age, of expectation and acceptance.

When Sandy and I first set foot on the island acreage that was to become our lasting home, a portion of it was a dispiriting miasma of logging slash and stumps. The tangled branches and limbs we could deal with by fire and axe and chainsaw, but the stumps, especially big Douglas fir stumps more than a metre in diameter, proved a formidable opponent. Some we blew out with explosives; some we battered out with an ancient bulldozer armed with a fearsome stump-splitter; still others we hacked out by hand, severing the roots with a mattock and winching the root mass out with a primitive come-along. The stumps were our nemesis, provoking a furiously physical response. We groaned with frustration when the brutes refused to budge and swaggered with self-satisfaction when at last a truculent stump surrendered to pulling and prying. For quite some time I entertained a fantasy of writing a book along the lines of a stump-puller's guide to the universe. Such was our level of absorption and absurdity.

Once the dust had settled over the stump ranch, there remained a half-dozen enormous western red cedar stumps within what was destined to become the garden. Most of them were already old by then, having been cut many decades earlier. On the sides of some, you could clearly see a notch into which loggers had inserted a springboard on which they'd stand to drop the giant tree using an axe and two-man saw.

Something—perhaps the whispering of benign spirits—urged that we leave these veterans alone, and so we did, laying out pathways and steps around their imposing bulk.

Over time their surfaces became weathered to an attractive silver, mottled with growths of lichens and mosses, and their rotting tops were colonized by western red huckleberries and salal, eventually forming lovely native hanging gardens. Rufous hummingbirds feed greedily on the tiny huckleberry flowers in spring and plump robins gorge on the ripe berries in summer. Songbirds took to nesting within the dense tangle of twigs. To prevent gangliness, I started shearing the stump-top huckleberry bushes into formal shapes—floating globes in one case, a solid square in another.

Beautiful in themselves, the stumps also make great structures for supporting other plants. We ran a spring-flowering clematis up the side of one tall stump and trained it into the huckleberry growing on top, so that the little blue bells of clematis blossoms are suspended among the graceful huckleberry twigs.

In a dark corner of the garden that sorely needed a bit of lighting up, we planted variegated Persian ivy at the base of two other stumps, one surmounted by a sheared crown of salal, the other by clipped huckleberries. The golden ivy leaves soon swathed the two trunks and in wintertime they gleam like twin pillars of hopefulness and cheer. Perhaps by way of a pièce de résistance, with one mighty stump we excavated its hollow centre and filled the cavity with topsoil in which we planted the contorted hazel known as Harry Lauder's walking stick. The little hazel thrived and, as already mentioned, now shows off its sinuous limbs from an elevated perch at which they can be seen to full advantage.

With these stumpy triumphs under our belts, we didn't hesitate several years ago when the opportunity arose to reach for the stars in stump gardening. After the catastrophic winter wind storms of 2006–2007, we'd judged it prudent to remove two huge but damaged cedars at the back of the garden. We had professionals take the trees down but leave the stumps to a height of about six metres—a choice deemed "really dumb" by one grizzled observer. Never mind, for within three years an established 'Kiftsgate' rose was reaching for the top of one stump and gives fair promise of smothering it entirely in white blossoms. At the base of its twin we planted a climbing hydrangea whose admittedly distant destiny too is to become a mighty tower of bloom.

As any gardener would, we take great satisfaction in this long, slow evolution from the strife and tumult of youth when stumps were our nemesis to the gentler joys now promoted by these graceful garden elements. I have become an ardent lover of stumps and can almost understand the enthusiasm some people manifest for those "realistic replica tree stumps" moulded from images of real trees in urethane or concrete.

Still, I prefer the real thing. I remember one old logger who visited our place and commended us for preserving the ancient stumps. "They're the sculptures of the coast," he told us. And while I pondered the irony of moving from "save the trees" to "save the stumps," I knew exactly what he meant.

Monomania

WITHIN THE GRAND mansion of gardening, there are any number of small closets and hidden corners in which odd practices occur. Among the more intriguing of these is what we might call monomaniacal gardening, this being an obsessive preoccupation with a single variety or species. It's widely acknowledged, for example, that rose fanciers may become obsessed with roses to the exclusion of everything else, including spouses and children, which is why rosarians should be taken out for a brisk walk and a stiff drink every once in a while. Unless a close watch is kept on them, certain devotees of dahlias are similarly apt to spiral down into complete exclusivity of interest, as are begonia growers and persons mesmerized by meconopsis.

These singular obsessions are not without merit and are certainly more commendable than, say, a fixation on Tom Cruise. Nevertheless, there is a subset among monomaniacal gardeners that does give cause for concern. These are people who have absolutely no interest in gardening itself, but tag along behind the ranks of bona fide gardeners solely to procure substances, often illegal, that plants produce.

Marijuana growers are the most obvious examples of the breed, and it's entirely possible to come upon pot cultivators of marvellous skill and dedication, expert in different varieties, geniuses at the manipulation of light and application of nutrients, adept at determining the precise nanosecond at which harvesting should occur for maximum effect. But suggest that they might also enjoy growing a few potatoes or cabbages, and they're apt to set the Rottweilers on you.

Then there was that case in the news not long ago in which a bold soul was apprehended for growing opium poppies in his urban yard. Rather than strategically scatter his crop among other less controversial flowers, this obsessive soul had his masses of *Papaver somniferum* lined up like army cadets behind chain-link fencing, with no other plant in sight, all but inviting the authorities to take an interest. A clear case of monomania entirely trumping common sense.

Another remarkable exposé of this mindset occurred a couple of years ago when the *Independent* newspaper in the United Kingdom published a story under the headline "Grow-Your-Own Viagra Craze Hits Britain's Garden Centres." The item detailed how a Berkshire allotment gardener named Michael Ford had stumbled upon the great realization that Viagra-like effects could be achieved by drinking a tea brewed from the blooms of winter-flowering heather. The gentleman was quoted as saying: "The effect was almost immediate. I had to stay in my potting shed for an hour or so before I could decently walk down the street."

The story went on to say that Ford contacted botanists specializing in the heather family at the Royal Botanic Gardens in Edinburgh, who confirmed that a Viagra-type chemical does indeed occur in the floral tissues of certain winter-flowering heathers, a particularly potent form being found in the alpine heather *Erica carnea*.

The quest for a "poor-man's Viagra" being something of a holy grail among a certain segment of the populace, involving elaborate experimentation with the likes of watermelon rinds, rotting eggs and red Tropea onions from Southern Italy, the *Independent* maintained that word of Ford's discovery had spread like wildfire. Garden centres were reportedly being besieged each weekend by persons eager to get into heather cultivation. Nurseries were unable to keep up with the demand. The paper quoted one spokesperson for a nursery chain saying, "We have had men buying dozens of the plants and, at one store in Croydon, there were men old enough to know better fighting over the last remaining trays."

The news item concluded with a final quote from a woman interviewed while shopping at a nursery in Dorking, who said: "It's amazing. My husband has never shown any interest in gardening before, but now he's out there night and day fussing over his heathers. Frankly, I preferred it when he left the garden to me and wasn't so frisky."

Apparently, response to the *Independent*'s article was as instant and enthusiastic as that of the people described in the story. Until, that is, it dawned upon the legions of newfound heather zealots that the *Independent*'s story had appeared on the first day of April. The whole thing was nothing more than an elegantly executed April Fool's Day joke.

Nevertheless, joke or no, the exercise does speak to deeper truths. Somewhere buried within the human psyche there must surely lurk an elemental instinct to find that singular plant of lasting happiness—

whether it's hapless Adam and Eve's tree of the knowledge of good and evil, or a pot of heather clasped by some little chap in Dorking desperate to reinvigorate his flaccid manhood.

It is an instinct for which we gardeners might keep careful watch, wary lest the heavy hand of monomania drag us also from our well-balanced plantings into the narrow confines of singular obsession.

Extreme Makeovers

I GREATLY ADMIRE those accomplished individuals who've got their gardens more or less "done." Oh sure, they may have the odd bit of tiddling-up to do every now and then, but their overall design and its component compositions are so firmly established and so unarguably correct they require no second guessing. The possessors of such gardens exude an enviable lightness of spirit and an air of easygoing confidence.

On the other hand, the rest of us—and, I would hazard a guess, the majority of us—prefer the extreme-makeover approach to garden design. We are never quite satisfied with things the way they are. Perfectionists in concept if not in execution, we are forever rearranging things, repositioning and reconfiguring, constantly tearing out underperformers and replacing them with promising new prospects.

Makeover mavens like ourselves are unfairly hampered in this work by various constraints. We have, for example, a remarkable capacity for underestimating the eventual size of certain plants while overestimating the mature dimensions of others. In our crowded beds, giants and pygmies jostle uncomfortably alongside one another. Ostensibly slender little specimens squeezed into a tight corner turn out to suffer from an unsuspected obesity and are soon squashing their neighbours sideways. Other reputedly more muscular customers are given a wide berth at planting time but quickly succumb to a form of botanic purging that reduces them to shivering little skeletons surrounded by expanses of bare dirt.

Another hazard: as a matter of principle we makeover artists have a great proclivity for ignoring instructions. "Does best in full sun" means nothing to us as we condemn the erstwhile sun lovers to the darkest corner of the yard. "Shows best in massed plantings" indicates to us that a solitary specimen is what's called for. In fact, the whole concept of massing and grouping smacks to us of grubby socialism whereas we prefer the rugged individualism of having one specimen of everything. Our hardscapes tend to be a bit soft around the edges and plain mushy in the middle. Our gardens are, in short, a dog's breakfast.

Which is precisely why an extreme makeover is occasionally called for. Like those eager but unimpressive persons featured on HGTV "reality shows," we long to see all our old rubbish torn out and replaced with sophisticated and enchanting plantings. But with no designer dudes to make the decisions for us, we're thrown back upon our own resources. The fact that all previous efforts have demonstrated conclusively that we have as much aptitude for garden design as for neurosurgery serves as no deterrent. We've read our magazines, we've watched our television shows, we've consulted experts and discussed with friends. We're as prepped as we can be. And we're stoked. We want a makeover and we want it now.

There are various schools of thought as to how to proceed. One perennial favourite is fashionable planning. You simply determine what's in vogue this year—maybe it's anything chartreuse or anything burgundy, maybe it's tussock grasses or epiphytes or all the plants named in Shakespeare's tragedies—and load up on these, scattering them where you will.

Whimsical planning is somewhat similar but more subjective. You couldn't care less what the madding crowd is mad for—you will follow your individual muse. Maybe you're an animal fancier as well as a gardener (not usually a salubrious mix) and will select only plants that are named after animals (an idea thoroughly entertained earlier in this volume). Or perhaps you'll want only plants that originate in countries you yourself have visited. Your garden will become a living map of your own life and travels. How utterly fascinating!

At our place, we tend toward another popular choice—seasonal planning. Surveying the estate in late autumn, we'll rhapsodize over anything still showing a hint of colour. A grumpy little fringe tree—which every summer we determine to tear out and replace with something finer—in fall turns such a gorgeous gold we decide to bring in more of them. Forget spring bulbs and mincing midsummer perennials, we want more burning bushes, more Persian parrotias, more berry-heavy pyracanthas. By spring, the perspective's turned inside out and the previous fall's planning appears the work of myopic dolts. Bring on the hellebores and hostas! Seasonal planning is one of the more effective ways of remaining in perpetual makeover mode.

But tearing out unwanted plants and replacing them with others can be a costly business and for many gardeners parsimonious planning becomes the order of the day. Here the notion is to cruise the nurseries for seasonal plant sales and clearance sections in order to scoop up plants on the sole criterion that they're cheap. Planning comes later, as you survey your yardful of withered bargains and ponder what possible configuration you can arrange them in. But it matters little, because delight derives not from the inherent beauty of the plant, nor from the comeliness of its arrangement, but rather from the bargain-basement price you paid for it.

All of these problematic planning paths lead to the same destination: the need for yet another makeover. To the contented gardener the prospect of repeatedly tearing the yard apart this way may seem entirely frightful. But those of us mad for makeovers know how much drama and passion they bring into your life. We'll makeover and over again until we can makeover no more.

Garden Gurus and Expert Avoidance

GARDENING IS A field of endeavour as rich in expertise as earthworms. Down every *allée,* behind every bit of boscage, there's an expert or two lying in wait for the opportunity to offer gardening advice. Some are generalists who know a little something about almost everything; ask them about *Asclepias* and they'll be as fully informed as when you quiz them on quince. Others are specialists who tend to know a tremendous amount about very little; they may be able to talk authoritatively for days about dahlias but be completely clueless as to cucumbers. All are generous to a fault in informing those of us who know next to nothing either about everything or about very little.

And this stands to reason because an expert requires a stock of uninformed gardeners among whom his expertise is both obvious and appreciated. If everyone were an expert, things would be far more difficult. Which is why a simmering resentment sometimes arises against people who aren't experts but feel the need to carry on as though they were. They'll sniff and snoot at other peoples' gardens, toss off a few botanical truisms in plummy tones and attempt a couple of tongue-twisting Latin names in a way that betrays they've been practising their pronunciation in the bathroom. These charlatans are quickly flushed from cover.

Far greater consternation is caused by people who do in fact possess a certain expertise but not the wisdom to know its limits. They may be perfectly sound on their soils, for example, and entirely reliable on propagation, but completely clueless on plant pathology. They couldn't tell a canker from a sap wart. Alas, puffed up to an exalted status, the demi-expert lacks the grace to utter the three words that separate knaves from the truly knowledgeable: "I don't know." Instead, he blusters and bluffs and insists upon things of which he knows nothing. The problem here is that he has proven himself so insightful in other areas that even an erudite gardener cannot hope to distinguish his good advice from bad.

The old adage that a little bit of knowledge is a dangerous thing rings particularly true in the garden.

A surfeit of knowledge, or at least of opinion, may be just as dangerous. Two or more experts going at it like bull elk in rut over what is or isn't required in a particular instance can give the inexpert gardener a head-pounding headache. One expert recommends a soil-preparation, fertilizing and watering scheme that radically differs from what a second pundit proposes. Both are eminent persons and you dare not fail to follow the advice of either. A third authority confirms neither of them but presents another approach entirely. You're left twisting in the wind of indecision.

Which brings us to the larger question of one's overall attitude to experts and their expertise. An immense spectrum of responses is available to us and, typically, you'll find avid gardeners populating every portion of the spectrum. At one extreme, you have persons determined to fawn over experts no matter what. Devoted followers, they go to the lectures, hanging on every word, chuckling dutifully at every witticism. They take copious notes. They never miss the expert's appearances on television and radio and in the print media. They buy their books. They twitter and tweet obsequiously. Rather than using the term "expert," they prefer the elevated "gardening guru," implying an almost spiritual discipleship. Any moment of crisis or indecision in the garden sends them swooning to their guru for advice and guidance.

On the opposite end of the spectrum, we find those rugged individualists with a sharply pointed instinct for expert avoidance. They've been gardening for thirty-five years, dammit, and they'll be providing dinner for the earthworms before they're gonna listen to a lot of silly prattle from some effete snob who's only studied it in books and never gotten out there and dirtied his hands in a garden of his own. Beneath this cranky exterior, as often as not there resides a soft spot, a place of vulnerability born of the perhaps unconscious recognition that if an expert describes precisely how best to perform a particular operation, you no longer have an excuse for not doing it properly. The expert avoider, schooled in the garden of hard knocks, is the ultimate outsider, an iconoclast, determined to do things his own way and the devil take the consequences.

It would be disingenuous of me not to confess that I'm on the borderline of skepticism myself. I believe the experience of having been thoroughly hoodwinked by religious extremists early in life rendered me subsequently incapable of ever again placing my trust in infallibility. I'm not proud of this, certainly, but console myself by taking occasional delight in instances where the pronouncements of a "guru" are later proven to be bunk. My skepticism has only been reinforced through the comedy of having myself being referred to as a "gardening guru" by certain dear but deluded persons. If a trifler like me can be accorded the appellation, why not everybody? And indeed across the vast geography of blogs and tweets almost everybody does have a definitive opinion, rendering the bona fide guru a threatened if not endangered species.

It goes without saying that a household composed of two or more gardeners who occupy fundamentally opposite places on the expertise spectrum is a household in trouble. To have a dissenter out in the yard in October grubbing away at the *Galanthus* while the devoted disciple is indoors receiving from her guru advice that early planting, certainly before the end of September, is an absolute requirement of *Galanthus* culture... here is a recipe for bitter recrimination on both sides.

In the interests of domestic harmony, then, perhaps we'd do best to advocate a "grain of salt" approach. We shall hear what the experts have to say, attempt to reconcile any discrepancies among them, sift out the rubbish of demi-experts and poseurs, and proceed at a stately pace in our own somewhat informed but essentially inexpert way.

The Pith of Garden Greatness

EVERY ONCE IN a while, a pensive plantsperson may set to wondering about what makes a garden truly remarkable. I was led to that fundamental question when asked to participate in a project involving the world's great gardens. There are books aplenty on the topic and enough websites to overwhelm even a casual browser. Naturally, the celebrated and famous names pop up—Sissinghurst and Stourhead, Giverny and Versailles, the Alhambra and Descanso Gardens. But what's at the pith of their greatness, if indeed they deserve that overworked superlative?

In the opinion of some, sheer size ranks high. There are those who will gush enthusiastically over Versailles, for example, but I am not among them. I've never visited the place and have little desire to do so. It's big enough, all right, overwhelmingly so, but its rigid formality strikes me as grimly repetitive. And the whole conception of the place—Louis XIV's petulant envy of another garden that he felt compelled to outdo—along with the wanton destruction of villages and farms to clear way for the garden, make it more a splendid monument to arrogance than an admirable achievement.

Defenders of Versailles might argue that its significance in the history of gardening entitles it to the appellation "great," and there's something to be said for this viewpoint. It's the basis upon which you'd include a masterpiece like Bagh-e Fin, created in the fourteenth century and now the oldest surviving garden in Iran. Perhaps its Safavid creators were every bit as repulsive as the Sun King, I don't know, leading us to wonder whether or not the ambitions and excesses of a garden's owner are inextricable from the success of the garden itself.

It's perhaps impolite to mention it, but nevertheless it remains the case that some of the splendid homes and gardens of Britain now drooled over by hordes of tourists were financed originally through proceeds from the West African slave trade. I like American gardening writer Frank McGourty's wry comment on the marvellous gardens designed by the iconic Englishwoman Gertrude Jekyll: "Miss Jekyll had her heyday at the height of the British Empire, when there was plenty of loose change around for the right people to have the right gardens." It's an abiding difficulty that many of the gardens typically designated as the world's greatest—whether that's the Villa Lante in Viterbo or the Lingering Garden at Suzhou—are the products of enormous wealth, not necessarily amassed in ethical ways. They are to gardening what castles are to architecture: drop-dead gorgeous, perhaps, but rather overwhelming, and belonging to another age.

Take Rousham House and Garden in Oxfordshire, for example. Designed in 1738 by the celebrated William Kent, it's a perfectly preserved example of the first phase of English landscape design, arguably England's greatest contribution to gardening. Wandering Rousham's meticulous landscape of trees and lawns threaded by rills and dotted with dramatically placed statuary, I did experience a delicious sense of peace, and this ability to induce a transcendental calmness of spirit is surely one of the attributes of a great garden. But, as the estate's brochure pointed out, the place is "frozen in time," a kind of horticultural museum.

My point is not that these splendid, albeit perhaps troubled, creations should be dismissed; I'm as eager as the next spade soldier to view what's most grand in humankind's history of gardening. Rather, it's to avoid the pitfalls of comparison. Neither to be goaded into trying to re-create Kew Gardens in the backyard, nor to be crestfallen that our own modest efforts are hopelessly second-rate compared with the Katsura Imperial Palace Garden.

Another American gardening writer, Henry Mitchell, had wise things to say on the topic: "Gardening is not some sort of game by which one proves his superiority over others, nor is it a marketplace for the display of elegant things that others cannot afford...It is not a monument or achievement, but a sort of traveling, a kind of pilgrimage...often a bit grubby and sweaty."

And that's part of it, I believe: the distinction between garden as object and gardening as activity. As much as we may admire the world's "great" gardens, I love best those in which the skill and passion of the individual gardener(s) shines through. A place in which, as Beth Chatto put it, there exists "an overall balance and harmony of shapes, form, outline and texture." Not splendour or opulence for their own sake, but a place skilfully designed, lovingly cared for, and in harmony with its environment.

In the end, I suppose, as with all art, we each come down to a subjective response as to how a particular garden leads *us* to feel. Am I overwhelmed by it? Depressed by it? Indifferent to it? Or do I find it charming, provocative, stimulative of altered consciousness?

Ultimately, a garden—whether monumental or minuscule—may be considered great insofar as most people who spend time in it experience their spirits rising and their imaginations blossoming in beauty.

Inclined toward the Vertical

WHETHER OBSERVED FROM the top looking down, the bottom looking up, or in the middle looking both up and down, a hillside garden can be immensely satisfying. And that's not surprising because hillsides and hollows have long been considered places of special magic; in art and literature we often find beauty lingering longest in the vale and dale, the glen and dell. This mythic beauty is what the hillside gardener seeks to emulate.

Remembering favourite gardens visited over the years, I find exhilarating hillsides springing readily to mind: magnificent Powis Castle in Wales with its enormous cloud hedges tumbling downhill, or Powerscourt Estate in Ireland, or on a more modest scale, the lovely Abkhazi Garden in Victoria. The Renaissance villas of Tuscany and certain of the temple gardens of Japan also derive their character as much from the hillsides they occupy as from their plantings and hardscapes. Former quarries—like those at Queen Elizabeth Park in Vancouver and the Butchart Gardens near Victoria—showcase how adventuresome gardening can transform even hopeless holes in the ground.

On a grand or tiny scale, wherever the surface of earth tends toward the vertical, even however slightly, advantages and opportunities accrue. A hillside accommodates cascading water, perhaps ending in a gentle pool or stream at its base. Or there may be a rock garden in which choice rocks and alpine plants miniaturize a mountain hillside. The brow of a hill provides an opportunity for certain plants to stand in striking silhouette against the sky and for certain others to be seen from underneath so that dangling catkins or pendulous blooms or elegantly contorted branches may be appreciated more fully. Other plants can drape languidly down a rock face to stunning effect.

Opportunities for viewpoints are an obvious gift of hills, as are microclimates and variations in moisture levels. And what shade-bedevilled gardener doesn't dream of a south- or southwest-facing slope? Such is the appeal, some people will go to extreme lengths to have a hill. I remember visiting a rather eccentric estate garden in West Cork, in which the owner (not an Irishman) had excavated a series of small lakes, then trucked the spoils up to form an artificial minimountain of dubious authenticity.

Less dramatically, our property is blessed with twin slopes that form a small valley through which a seasonal stream flows. The western-facing slope is in Douglas fir woodlands, a wild garden of great natural charm. On the opposite side, our garden cascades down the gentle east-facing slope. We've terraced it with local sandstone dry walls, creating four levels of elevation, terracing being the time-honoured method of preventing erosion and facilitating hillside watering. The low walls, besides being pleasing in themselves, allow *Aubretia* and *Arabis* and spreading *Dianthus* to drape lazily down them.

Certain plants will thrive in the higher and dryer conditions on the upper levels but might fail miserably farther down. For example, we've never lost a Japanese maple planted along the higher reaches, but have seen several succumb presumably to wet winters in the damper ground below. The smoke bushes, *Cotinus,* similarly don't like having wet feet. We've got a cluster of them, both purple and green, at the top of the slope, where their "smoke" gets brilliantly backlit by the western sun. Being above us on the hill, the bushes appear far larger than they actually are, and this is another trick of hillside gardening: that the dimensions and relationships of plants can be manipulated by their positioning.

Of course, there are drawbacks to the hillside garden. Wheelbarrow access can be a problem. Making your way to the top of the hill, only to discover you've forgotten some tool or other necessary to the task at hand, if repeated enough times, can become vexing. Weeding, pruning and similar chores may sometimes be unduly arduous on a steep slope. I remember meeting a gracious old gardener in New Zealand who'd developed a spectacular small garden down an almost-impossible rock face. She liked to joke that she had one leg far shorter than the other from working so long on that slope.

I won't go so far as to say that hillside gardeners are a breed apart, but there's no question that the particular challenges and opportunities offered by hillsides, and the ingenuity with which so many gardeners transform even dreary slopes into places of particular beauty, earn the hillside garden a distinctive niche in the pantheon of great gardens.

Seeing the Light

"TEXTURE AND LIGHT are the fundamentals of garden design." So said John Wills as he showed a small group of us around Trelinnoe Park, his masterful "garden of landscape," whose thirty acres occupy a corner of the twenty-eight hundred acres of his sheep and cattle ranch in New Zealand. Everything in the garden—the many hundreds of trees, the several large ponds, the occasional expanse of lawn—was planned in accordance with John's analysis of light. When making design decisions he would, he told us, walk the grounds in morning and evening to study the angles and qualities of light so that plantings could be arranged to take best advantage of it.

This is an insight that photographers and painters perhaps appreciate more thoroughly than gardeners. The great American photographer Edward Steichen said of his early years of photographing natural scenes: "I knew, of course, that trees and plants had roots, stems, bark, branches, and foliage that reached up toward the light. But I was coming to realize that the real magician was light itself." Indeed, and this is a magician with whom the gardener is equally well advised to work. Although not emphasized in gardening manuals as much as it might be, dexterous manipulation of the play of light within a garden can make all the difference between a rather average and an especially fine effect. The right plant in the right place and the right light.

The business is complicated by the tremendous variations in light. The brilliant big-sky sunlight of prairie country differs markedly from the diffuse light of a misty coastal forest. Within a single location, the quality of light shifts as the angle of sunlight rises and falls with the seasons. A similar modulation occurs within each day, as the long slanting rays of morning gradually give way to the brighter, harder glint of midday and then soften again in the more golden glow of late afternoon. As the great British colourist Penelope Hobhouse wrote, "Even the simplest specimen tree shading a green lawn conveys a constantly changing pattern of colour as the light alters from minute to minute, and as the seasons modulate the tones of the leaves."

Hobhouse recalls how she dealt with the light-related challenges faced in designing a small and shaded town garden. "In the corner of deepest shade I used only green foliage plants, strong in leaf form and textural interest, many of them evergreen but complemented in season with white flowers." In a somewhat sunnier area, she "stressed the different mood by growing shrubs with golden leaves and flowers of pale yellow to give at least the illusion of sunlight."

This is what the light-wise gardener does: conjure illusions and special effects by locating plants where they'll play most appealingly with a certain light. We have some hint of that at our place when, on clear springtime mornings, shafts of lucid sunlight illuminate the flowers and unfurling leaves of several crabapple trees in such a way that a green and golden radiance seems to emanate from within the leaves themselves, creating the semblance of a natural candelabra. We get a similar effect when late-afternoon sunlight—seeming mellower than its sprightly morning counterpart—streams through the foliage of a weeping willow pendant above a small pond. The illuminated leaves trace a calligraphy of green-gold beauty above the gilded shimmer of the pond. Late-afternoon sunlight candent on the trunks of old Douglas firs transforms their furrowed bark from lacklustre grey to a pleasingly reddish tone. For us, few plants catch the westering sun more thrillingly than golden hops, *Humulus lupulus* 'Aureus', whose dense clusters of large yellow leaves glow vividly in the golden hours.

Backlighting is one of the gardener's favourite effects, especially employing late-afternoon sunshine to illuminate certain plants from behind. The smoke bushes, *Cotinus,* are all excellent in this regard, with their ethereal halos of minutely threaded "smoke" shown to best effect when the setting sun shines through them. The same is true for the feathery foliage of our 'Skyline' gleditsia that glows with western sunlight like floating golden clouds. The flower heads of tall ornamental grasses like *Stipa gigantea,* and of the plume poppy, *Macleaya cordata,* as well as the silky seedheads of certain clematis vines, are all effective in much the same way.

Some leaves perform beautifully in a variety of seasonal lighting schemes. The leaves of the copper beech—I think, actually, of all beeches—have a special knack for capturing sunlight and breezes so as to create almost liquid compositions of light. Even in the middle of winter, lowly *Bergenia* shows to marvellous effect when pale sunlight shining directly on the leaves burnishes them to polished copper.

The great American landscape photographer Ansel Adams used to speak of "translucent truth," by which I think he meant the perception of another reality, a revelation beneath the surface of things, seen through their illumination. This is what the gardener too strives for, in collaboration with that cunning magician, light itself.

Whiteout Conditions

ON A PERFECTLY sunny midsummer morning not long ago I saw a dazzling vision of white. In the foreground, a cluster of herbaceous peonies lifted their sumptuous white pompoms into the air like giddy cheerleaders after a touchdown. Close beside them stood a milky-white inflorescence of faithful old bellflowers, *Campanula lactiflora*. On the terrace level behind and above, a congregation of white fireweed, *Epilobium angustifolium* f. *album,* held aloft their upright tapers of snowy small flowers. Off to the right, the brilliant ivory bracts of a Korean dogwood, *Cornus kousa* 'Chinensis', and the massed white lacecap flowers of a climbing *Hydrangea petiolaris* amplified the effect. On a still-higher terrace, the tiny white flowers of a greater sea kale, *Crambe cordifolia,* floated like mist above the others. And, highest of all, a great tumbling cumulus of white on a rangy mock orange completed a near-perfect composition.

I use the term "composition" rather loosely because nobody had ever sat down and said: "Now look here, if we plant each of these specimens just so, they'll eventually combine to brilliant effect." No diagrams or ground plans were involved, no digital mock-ups of eventual outcomes. Those are the kind of things accomplished garden designers do. The rest of us more or less muddle along until, occasionally, serendipity perhaps takes things into her own hands and voila! A genuine small stroke of genius.

Any number of unrelated factors may conspire toward, or against, a particular effect. For example, the spring preceding this midsummer vision had been a strangely extended season, remaining cool and cloudy right through into July, during which plant schedules were entirely topsy-turvy. In general, everything seemed to straggle along about three weeks behind. Certainly the peonies were very tardy, as the latest-flowering types are typically finished blooming by summer solstice. The *Cornus kousa,* a late-blooming dogwood anyway, was several weeks behind herself. The white fireweed, on the other hand, seemed to have ignored the inclement weather and bloomed on time, comfortably ahead of its more familiar carmine-pink cousins.

Given to us originally by an accomplished gardening friend and fellow islander named Rosemary Talbot (why do so many gardeners have such floricultural names?), the fireweeds seemed rather lacklustre for their first few years, pale and fragile as an anemic child. I was tempted to make dismissive remarks about them, deriding misguided plant breeders for leaching the colour and scent and vibrancy out of already perfectly evolved plant forms. (Indignation born of ignorance is a dreadful menace, and it was only later that I came to learn that white fireweed is a rare but naturally occurring form, like the spirit bear, and one of the great beauties of far-northern landscapes.) Sure enough, this past spring, in their own good time—after a fairly brutal winter that may have warmed them with intimations of their northern homeland—they emerged from the earth with a real sense of purpose, throwing off any vestiges of pallor, slender but vigorous white beauties that put to shame my misguided discourtesy toward the hybridizers.

The greater sea kale experienced a similar narrative arc. We originally planted a clump of it in the lower garden where it would grow vigorously every spring, producing large dark leaves rather like rhubarb. A member of the cabbage family, and prone to diseases such as clubroot that frequently afflict the family, it would produce dozens of slender flowering stems of which most would systematically wilt, blacken and die just before the flowers opened. Undaunted, we planted a second specimen on higher, drier, stonier ground where only the hardiest of hardy perennials might thrive. Naturally, it's done splendidly and its spectacular inflorescence of tiny white flowers now reaches two metres high and almost as wide, resembling a giant *Gypsophila*.

We have no idea where the rangy mock orange came from and I prefer to imagine it's a *Philadelphus trichothecus*, a British Columbia native, that has wandered in of its own accord.

As with the fireweed, the peonies appeared to have benefitted from the good deep freeze of that particular winter. So it's entirely possible that the peonies, campanula, fireweed, sea kale, dogwood, mock orange and hydrangea have never before been simultaneously at the height of their flowering and may never be so again.

Lastly, I experienced my rapturous vision of white while reclining in our new sunroom that provides a view of the garden not available elsewhere. The multispecies ribbon of white I saw from that viewpoint did not have quite the same impact from any other perspective in the garden.

So it was a fluid composition at best, a configuration of accidents and incidents that may or may not recur, and all the more precious for that.

Carved in Stone

ON DISMAL WINTER days, the value of ornaments in the garden—statues, figures, urns and the like—becomes ever more apparent, reminding us that the artistry of the gardener and of the sculptor have gone hand in hand through human history, together creating the brilliant collaborations admired in the world's finest gardens. "Statues," wrote garden-design aficionado Sylvia Crowe, "are the great humanizers, by which man projects his personality and his love of creation into the realm of nature."

Such high-blown ideals of garden artistry can be somewhat strained as we rummage through the concrete and cast stone figures at garden-supply centres searching for that perfect piece of statuary while discreetly gasping at the price tags. Even if we were to find an appropriate piece at a not-impossible price, purists like Ms. Crowe would scarcely be impressed. "Since sculpture is an expression of the creative spirit of man," she advises, "each work, to keep its value, must retain its individuality. Its force is lost if imitations are mass produced, however good the original may have been. The interest of a focal point is gone as soon as it is realized that it is but one more copy of the Mercury which we have seen in a dozen other gardens."

Oh dear. What's a person to do? Short of becoming an accomplished sculptor oneself, or a millionaire, perhaps the best fallback strategy is to curry favour with sculptors in the community. This is less daunting a task than might at first be thought and may involve only a modicum of grovelling. Sculptors exist in abundance and, like their co-conspirators the gardeners, are a curious breed of outsiders driven to pursue their art whether or not society encourages them to do so. Like gardeners, sculptors are anxious that their work be seen and appreciated. Nor, like gardeners, do they usually have sufficient space for their accumulating creations. Lastly—and this is perhaps the crucial consideration—just as gardeners compulsively bestow plants on anyone who lingers for a moment in their garden, sculptors too like to give their stuff away.

Chronically undervalued and underpaid, as are most artists and gardeners, sculptors seem to respond not in bitterness but in munificence.

Thus it has come to pass that our own modest little garden has been esthetically elevated by a number of sculptures that worked their way into the grounds through the generosity of local sculptors. One year, we returned home from a weekend away and were startled to find a giant stone banana slug on the patio. A metre in length, sculpted from native sandstone, and polished to a preternatural smoothness by wildlife artist Peter Karsten, the recumbent slug figure had been mischievously brought into the garden under cover of darkness and placed for maximum shock effect. There it remains, a smoothly beautiful and playful reminder of our interactions with other garden creatures.

A second piece arrived in more stately fashion. Local sculptor Michael Dennis, known for his larger-than-life wooden figures rendered from huge pieces of old-growth western red cedar felled, regrettably, in coastal clear-cuts, gave a sculpture to Sandy on her fiftieth birthday. Titled *Spirit of the Garden,* it's a woman's figure sculpted from Vancouver Island granite, a beautifully textured medium that undergoes subtle changes in colour with the shifting sunlight. Given pride of place, both graceful and ancient in appearance, she casts an unmistakable spell across the garden, and in winter, as her surrounding vegetation dies away, she seems to grow in stature and in power.

Another life-sized piece came to us through the Denman Island Home and Garden Tour. One year, certain properties on the tour were assigned a specific local artist whose works would be displayed in that garden, and we were pleased to welcome Richard Menard, a sculptor in both wood and stone who also works primarily with western red cedar. He installed half-a-dozen large wooden figures throughout our gardens, to the great benefit of the gardens and delight of tour goers. Afterwards, he left one behind, as he said, "for the garden." Sculpted in red cedar salvaged from a beach at Clayoquot Sound and titled *Mataji,* it depicts the Hindu mother goddess and consort to Shiva swathed in a smoothly carved shawl. From her perch above a stone alcove, she gazes out with a tranquility one hopes suffuses the garden generally.

What I especially like about these pieces, beyond their epitomizing the generosity of their donors, is that all are created from local materials— sandstone, granite and red cedar—by local artists with a contemporary sensibility. They embody the genius of this particular place and time in a way that, for example, polished marble statuary from an Italian villa garden, with all its excellence, never really could. Equally at home here as native plants, these figures nestle into the garden while projecting, as Sylvia Crowe put it, a human personality and love of creation into the realm of nature.

Scents and Sensibilities

"THE FLOWER OF sweetest smell is shy and lowly," Wordsworth observed, and nowhere is this more true than among the peculiar little flowers of shrubs grown primarily for their winter scent. We have, or have had, several such shrubs in the yard, gawky customers most of them, with flowers that range in appearance from insignificant to mildly ridiculous. But their powerful fragrances, broadcast at a time of year when pollinating insects are at a premium, provide a redeeming succession of scents to lift poor spirits sagging beneath filthy weather.

First to flower for us—often before Christmas in milder winters—is *Viburnum × bodnantense* 'Dawn'. One of several winter-flowering viburnums, 'Dawn' or 'Pink Dawn' is a deciduous shrub that can grow up to three metres tall. Its deeply veined leaves colour nicely in autumn, then fall off, exposing a rather scruffy-looking skeleton that leads you to think that if viburnums were allowed to hang out on street corners wearing hoodies, this one probably would. Depending on local conditions, the shrub blooms between November and April, producing loose clusters of small flowers that open white with a strong pink flush. Although bedraggled-looking in foul weather, perched forlornly on their bare twigs, the little flowers are intensely aromatic, especially when brought indoors to warmth. When I remember to, I prune the bush after blooming to limit its gangliness. With care, it can be grown in zone six, but even in our milder winters the flower buds may be killed by a bad cold snap.

By mid-January we often start catching intoxicating whiffs from a little Himalayan sarcococca growing just outside the front door. If we could have only one winter-flowering plant, this would be my choice for it is altogether admirable. It's a reasonably handsome evergreen shrub, or sub-shrub, seldom even a metre tall. Spreading by underground runners, in ideal conditions it can stretch nearly three metres wide. We have it tucked in by our entryway in full sun—both for the plant's protection, and so we can enjoy the scent whenever passing in or out—but it reputedly performs well even in deep shade, and can be very useful under low-branching evergreens or overhangs. Unlike the bare-twigged scenters, this bushy little customer sports glossy green leaves that remain attractive in all seasons. Right at the very gloomiest time of year, rows of tiny white flowers open, somewhat hidden on the undersides of the arching twigs. The flowers are like winter's equivalent of summer's evening-scented stocks—inconspicuous little things able to cast a perfume of prodigious potency. Continuing for many weeks, this is a scent that sets the soul to rejoicing, a fragrance that instantly sweeps the imagination away from the foul dreariness of January, off to someplace balmy, exotic and benign. It's like the poor person's winter getaway, without the crush of airports, lost luggage and jostling for a spot on the beach. The variety we have, *Sarcococca hookeriana* var. *humilis,* is native to the Himalayas and listed as hardy to zone five. If you can grow it, grow it.

Hardly has the scent of sarcococca faded than the February daphne opens its little rosy-purple blooms. Deciduous and growing to just over a metre tall, this is another gawky and stiff-twigged shrub. High-strung like all the daphnes, it is not quite as temperamental as the evergreen winter daphne, which, as one of our manuals puts it, is "so much loved, so prized for its pervasive, pre-spring fragrance that it continues to be widely planted in spite of its unpredictable behaviour." Native to Europe, the February daphne, *D. mezereum,* has naturalized in parts of the eastern United States. True to its name, it blooms for us in February, before leafing out, and the flowers persist well into spring, followed by small red berries that, like the plant itself, are poisonous to humans, though not to birds.

For years the last of our fragrant bare-twigged beauties to bloom was the Chinese witch hazel, *Hamamelis mollis,* that graceful vase-like shrub with long snaking branches and roundish felted leaves. It produced bold golden-yellow flowers along its twigs, as visually pleasing as they are fragrant. However, it is the least hardy of the available types, and an exceptionally cold winter killed our fine specimen outright. We have not thought to replace it, even though in colder places, the same scent can be had from a group of hybrids called *H.* × *intermedia,* which are crosses of Chinese and Japanese witch hazels. Although smaller, their flowers have the same distinctive petals, dangling like little ribbons, though in coppery reds and oranges less conspicuous than the pure yellow.

Soon afterwards, the scents of hyacinth and narcissus and violet will be perfuming the air, and the wild rush of early spring will engulf us. But not so tipsily that we forget the shy and lowly little flowers whose transcendent scents have carried us so faithfully through the worst of winter.

AND IN THE END

Plantsman, Heal Thyself

ENTRENCHED GARDENERS RECOGNIZE that gardening and healthfulness go together like tomatoes and basil. The activities of gardening—the endless bending and stooping and twisting and reaching—constitute a conditioning workout that combines the finer elements of tai chi, aerobics and mixed martial arts. Plus, no one who gardens can for a minute doubt that working with seeds and soil and plants is a far more effective method of reducing stress and tension than is gobbling questionable pharmaceuticals. And, of course, the regular consumption of fresh, organic, homegrown fruits, vegetables and herbs is at the very pith of healthful living.

But there's another, perhaps less obvious, aspect to the conjunction of gardens and healthfulness. Here I mean the garden's capacity to assist in overcoming illness or pain, what we might call the ameliorative and restorative powers of a garden. I can speak on this matter with an unaccustomed authoritativeness because I've recently had first-hand experience in the field. For most of my life, I've been one of those annoying persons who seldom get sick and generally radiate robust vigour. However, after six decades of largely uninterrupted healthfulness, except for the occasional broken bone or torn muscle, I finally came a cropper when a congenital heart defect required open-heart surgery.

Receiving this unwelcome diagnosis, I allowed myself a decently brief period of self-pity and then, as any gardener would, got down to the necessary work to prepare for the business at hand. Knowing that I faced at least a week in hospital and a further month or more in convalescence, I realized I needed to accumulate a store of garden impressions that I might call upon in the dark hours ahead, much as we savour the gardens of summer as tonic against the gloom of winter. I took to strolling the early-spring garden, listening to favourite music on headphones, associating music with the beauty of the place, so that when I replayed it in my dreary hospital ward I might experience the garden again in imagination.

There is no doubt in my mind that maintaining these soothing visions of beauty helped enormously in reducing stress and anxiety as I lay on the hospital gurney under bright lights awaiting the anaesthetist's oblivion. Or afterwards, returned from the brink, spending long hours in the sensory deprivation of the hospital. As soon as I was ambulatory, I made a regular beeline to the small but lovely hospital garden where I felt real healing commence, notwithstanding the fact that the only other people I ever saw in the garden were smokers seeking a place to light up. After three weeks of confinement—I'd suffered a mysterious "setback" that prolonged the ordeal—I returned home, heartsore but healing. Within hours of getting back to terra firma and real food, my spirits were soaring. Yes, to be back amid blossoms and songbirds, exulting in the garden's capacity to help heal and restore us to our true selves.

I offer this personal anecdotal testimony not in a vacuum, but as part of a growing body of evidence concerning the importance of gardens in the healing arts. In a paper titled "Health Benefits of Gardens in Hospitals" delivered at the Plants for People conference at the International Exhibition Floriade 2002, Roger S. Ulrich of Texas A&M University pointed out that for more than a thousand years both Western and Asian medical traditions maintained the belief that plants and gardens are beneficial to patients. However, in our society, that traditional wisdom was jettisoned in the early decades of the 1900s, when advances in medical science led to hospital design that focused on new medical technology and infection risk, in many cases eliminating hospital gardens.

More recent developments in mind-body medical science are now shifting emphasis back to incorporate aspects of traditional medicine, including the use of gardens for healing environments. As Professor Ulrich put it: "The fact that there is limited but growing scientific evidence that viewing gardens can measurably reduce patient stress and improve health outcomes has been a key factor in the major resurgence in interest internationally in providing gardens in hospitals and other healthcare facilities."

The studies he cites really are quite remarkable, indicating that for recuperating patients, having views of gardens has been clinically shown—through beneficial changes in blood pressure, heart activity, muscle tension, and brain electrical activity—to elevate levels of positive feelings, such as pleasantness and calm, while reducing negatively toned emotions such as fear, anger and sadness. Furthermore, not only were patients who enjoyed garden views less anxious during the post-operative period than those who didn't, but also they actually suffered less pain, shifting faster than other groups from strong narcotic pain drugs, and tended to have shorter hospital stays.

If these findings are true for the populace at large, how much more so for passionate gardeners, as I discovered myself—lying immobile but remembering past loveliness when no other was available, then savouring a garden when it was at hand, all the while dreaming of healthfulness and beauty still to come.

Storm Clouds on the Horizon

ON THOSE OCCASIONS when what Gertrude Jekyll called "the time of perfect young summer" is upon us, our thoughts naturally incline toward the more tranquil and sublime aspects of gardening. Sunshine and nesting songbirds, unfurling blossoms and emerging butterflies form such a joyful panorama we almost forget the other side of the garden—that dark corner where disaster lurks, awaiting the chance to strike.

I don't mean the occasional mishap or irritating inconvenience: a broken waterline or sudden wilting in the clematis. Nor even a major blunder, such as hiring a recommended arborist who—once set loose among your trees—morphs into a demented wood butcher. These are merely the commonplace vicissitudes of the gardening life, and hardened gardeners, after the requisite grumbling and growling, can handle them, no problem.

When we talk about disaster in the garden, we mean a thorough roughing-up, the like of which hasn't been seen in decades. Arctic air of such sustained and bone-chilling intensity it gets old-timers recalling how regularly Niagara Falls used to freeze solid, and now threatens to obliterate the half-hardy specimens you've spent ages establishing. Winds so ferocious they slash and pummel everything in their path like a frenzied mob drunk on ancient enmities. Rain, relentless and enduring rain, that has you surfing the web for ark blueprints. Scorching heat and sustained drought that portend desertification.

Having for decades ignored scientific warnings about an approaching climate-change crisis, the daily news now churns with tales of calamity and ruination, cataclysms of biblical magnitude, many of them afflicting the most vulnerable populations on earth. Hurricanes Katrina and Sandy, monster cyclones in the Philippines or wildfires in Australia. While nowhere near as terrorizing as those catastrophes, several recent winter storms on the BC south coast, most notably the tempest that wreaked havoc among the trees of Vancouver's Stanley Park, have given us enough of a knock on the head to realize what a bona fide disaster might look like. And if the climatologists are to be believed—not an easy leap of faith, I grant you, given the forecasting travails of their meteorologist companions down the corridor—the age of great storms driven by global climate change is now upon us.

In light of this reality—rather than hypothesis—more gardeners may begin bending their efforts to what in a weak moment we could call the global-warming garden. This is not a matter of cultivating banana trees in Whitehorse, but rather of rethinking our gardens for radically altered circumstances. Many gardeners are already well under way, employing waterwise gardening, permaculture, forest gardening and various other organic methods that both enhance a garden's resilience and minimize its contribution to climate change. Refinements might include land contouring to deal with exceptional rain events and a pruning regime that minimizes tree and shrub damage from heavy snowfalls, ice storms and hurricane-force winds. Our choice of plants might similarly be guided by considerations of how well they can withstand heavy snow, ice or violent wind as well as extended drought.

And perhaps some psychological fine-tuning might be in order as well. Since time immemorial, gardeners have developed a refined sense of indignation at the vicissitudes inflicted on them by capricious weather. There's a long and distinguished tradition of lamenting droughts, floods, frosts and winds as afflictions sent specifically to torment the gardener. But if we are indeed now beginning to reap the whirlwinds of our profligate lifestyles, perhaps some tweaking of our instinctive reaction to bad weather is in order. Would it help, do you think, if we could view a rampageous gust of wind that flattens our prized *Magnolia grandiflora* not as a cruel twist of fate but the logical consequence of our repeated car trips to Las Vegas? Just think of the added gratification to be had from kicking and cursing the leaf blower, not only because it won't start (again) but also because its fumes are directly responsible for the drought that's killed the cedar hedge.

On a more constructive note, I wonder if the fine tradition gardeners have, along with farmers, fisher folk, and the like, of withstanding the consequences of foul weather, doesn't put us in a somewhat stronger position to face whatever perturbations lie ahead. The spirit of gardening, that spunkiness that gets us up and outdoors to gather the debris and set things right as soon as the tempest has abated, may be more and more in demand as abnormal weather becomes the norm. On brighter days—like those among the pleasures of a perfect young summer—I've somewhat less doubt that the ingenuity and adaptability of gardeners in the age of global warming will surmount and eventually transform whatever disasters await us.

Altered Fates

HARDENED GARDENERS ARE FULLY aware that they are the playthings of the Fates. And that the Fates are a capricious bunch to deal with. The unpredictabilities of climate, the contrary predilections of plants, and the overall dominance of chaos theory in matters horticultural all contribute to the precariousness of the gardening life. It's within that context I'm remembering the vicious cold snaps of a particular winter that decimated so many of our marginally hardy plants—a dozen mature *Nandina domestica* and a venerable *Mahonia × media* 'Charity' destroyed to the roots; a veteran *Ceanothus* killed outright; euphorbias, Spanish brooms, sarcococcas blasted. Penny-ante problems compared with the deprivations and violences on display around the planet, of course, but nevertheless a time of loss and lamentation.

Among these frightful events, we were compelled to witness the dismaying death and decomposition of our prized *Aeoniums*. For the past dozen years or more, we'd coddled these tender succulents, growing them in large pots on the patio in summertime and hauling them into the unheated greenhouse for overwintering. Admittedly, they have no business being here, as they're native to the balmy Atlantic coasts of Morocco and the Canary Islands, and are frost tolerant to only minus four degrees Celsius. We also saw them growing handsomely as elegant shrubs in New Zealand gardens. But who could resist such tropical-looking beauties with their succulent rosettes of fleshy leaves. Not us. We grew two hybrids of *Aeonium arboreum*—'Atropurpureum', which has jade-green leaves when grown in shade but darkens to maroon purple in full sun; and 'Zwartkop', whose lustrous dark-purple leaves shine almost black. Flourishing enthusiastically in their patio pots, they were a highlight of the garden and sure to attract the attention of visitors.

When that particular winter's cold-blooded Arctic outflows sent temperatures plummeting all along the south coast, I fired up an electric heater in the greenhouse and on the most severe nights covered the shivering aeoniums with sheets. But to no avail. The succulents shrivelled to a miserable state, appearing to melt like plastic flowers on a desert parking lot. At the slightest touch, their blighted leaves fell from the stems. The stench of death hung over them. Observing our beauties dying before our eyes and powerless to prevent it, Sandy and I accepted this bitter turn of events with that mixture of sadness and resignation familiar to weather-bedevilled gardeners everywhere. We spoke philosophically about the transitoriness of life, recalled anew how Nature bats last. Reluctantly, we concluded that we would grow aeoniums no more.

No sooner had the icy weather retreated to its northern redoubt than it was time to clean out the greenhouse for spring planting. I started hauling away the aeonium corpses, still withered in their pots. Their shrivelled and rotted roots came out of the soil with barely a tug. But, hold on here! Mid-job I noticed that, although the stems were wizened and lifeless along their entire length, some of the topmost tips still had a bit of greeny life in them. It was as though the plants had withdrawn whatever remaining vital energy they possessed and stored it, not in their roots as most plants would, but in their extremities, roughly the equivalent of a human body dying everywhere except in its toes and fingertips.

Now we were in a pretty pickle indeed. Should I carry on disposing of the corpses, true to our considered resolve to quit growing high-maintenance and heart-breaking aeoniums, or should I seek to snatch victory from the jaws of Death by pruning off and rooting these promising tips and thereby perhaps consign us to further years of heaving heavy pots in and out of the greenhouse and living in repeated dread of another winter die-off? Needless to say, it was no contest. For almost any gardener, the remote possibility of cultivating something desirable entails the inescapability of attempting it. Chiding myself for the fool I was, I snipped off several dozen of the last-gasp tips and rooted them in refreshed soil in the very pots in which their family tree had so disastrously shrivelled.

Sure enough, almost every one of the cuttings struck. And, having struck, flourished through the summer months, so that we were soon back to as many plants as we'd had pre-disaster. (Raven-black 'Swartzkop' was unhappily not among the born-again, which I especially regretted because it was given to us originally by the great gardener and writer Helen Chesnut.) Our previous philosophical musings on life and death in the garden subsequently underwent the necessary amendments and revisions.

For several more years I trundled the pots back into the greenhouse every autumn, nattering tiresomely about how much more cumbersome they were becoming. The aeoniums would crouch inside, trying their best to withstand months of cold and damp, all the while no doubt dreaming of the warm breezes of the Canary Islands. No matter; come spring, they'd regain their vitality and flesh out for a fine summer show. Then, in due course, another spiteful winter hit us and once again the aeoniums collapsed in a melodramatic swan song. Could they be brought back from near death yet again? Possibly. Was I willing to go through the effort another time, and perhaps innumerable times thereafter? Not really. With heavy hearts, we let them go. I miss them still. And as I ponder this tale of born-again aeoniums, considering their situation and our own, I'm certain I can hear the Fates chuckling among themselves over the great bit of fun they've once again enjoyed at our expense.

Out of Control

GARDENERS ARE, ALMOST by definition, controlling personalities. Author Merilyn Simonds writes: "Because it was the first thing we enclosed and made our own, the garden has become a symbol of the human penchant for control." Amid the chaos of life at large, the garden offers a small repository of order and good governance, a delineated space within which the assembled elements can be judiciously placed and painstakingly nurtured to achieve their full potential.

So it stands to reason that a significant portion of the gardener's work lies in the exercise of control, in its continual reassertion against the elements of disruption and upheaval. Underachieving plants are poked and prodded into improved performance. Ill-disciplined specimens are sheared and clipped and pruned and, when necessary, rudely hacked at in order that they be brought back into line. Our intolerance of insubordination means that delinquent plants, those that consistently refuse to conform to the garden's strict code of conduct, are eventually and quite properly expelled like miscreant schoolboys.

We place a premium upon vegetative docility, reserving our fondest affections for varieties most amenable to discipline. These enjoy the perks of our approval, being accorded pride of place and shown to admiring visitors. Plants that toe the party line are rewarded with more than their fair share of water and nutrients. If there's a precious bit of compost to be allocated, who do you think will receive it, the compliant beauty or the balky underachiever?

Booting out the delinquents and cosseting the goody two-shoes, that's the disciplinarian gardener's way of running a tight ship. There are hazards involved, of course, as there are in most endeavours. A very fine line divides well-ordered gardens from the plant-by-number landscapes found outside certain commercial establishments. The most extreme example of authoritarian gardening I ever encountered was a garden managed by a retired engineer in which every plant was clipped, restrained and aligned into rows so precise they would have made a drillmaster drool. I instantly thought of the rows of us good little Catholic school-kids lined up beneath the disapproving glare of Mother Superior.

This is why weeds so get on our nerves. They are entirely intractable, forever popping up where least wanted, obstinately refusing to be dis-lodged, perversely seeding and spreading like an insurrection. Weeds are hooligans massing at the garden gate, determined to overrun us and confound all our efforts. Sensing their menace, we fight back with hoe and weed whacker and, once desperation has set in, with furtive spraying of herbicide. Perhaps the weeds withdraw temporarily, and we are lulled into a false complacency that good order has been restored. Fools that we are.

Certain creatures seem similarly insidious, forever attempting to gnaw away at the established order of things. They come creeping and crawling into our trim and tidy quarters, vermin of all sorts, parasites and gluttonous larvae stuffing themselves with precious fruits and foli-age. Incorrigible squirrels, disgusting tent caterpillars, marauding star-lings—they've not a shred of respect for the rule of law or the divine rights of property.

Small wonder we get twitchy listening to the mewlings of those who advocate including unruly flora and fauna in our gardens. Giant hogweed, for God's sake! Oh yes, there's no end of well-intentioned but starry-eyed naïfs willing to champion the cause of biological anarchy. Diversity they call it, as though that explained everything. They'll quote Gerard Manley Hopkins at you: "Long live the weeds and the wilderness yet." Fair enough, but how about they live long someplace other than in my little garden? Or get this from Nathaniel Hawthorne: "There is perhaps a sort of sacredness about [weeds]. Perhaps, if we could pene-trate Nature's secrets, we should find that what we call weeds are more essential to the well-being of the world than the most precious fruit or grain." Now, much as one might admire the dark romanticism of *The Scarlet Letter* or *The House of the Seven Gables,* I really can't accept the suggestion that something as pernicious as trailing blackberry is more "essential to the well-being of the world" than my kohlrabi.

Still, you have to play along with these idealists if you want to stay out of trouble these days. If it's been decreed that gardens should have weeds and weevils, who are we to raise a fuss? Never rock the botanical boat, I say, unless you're prepared to get your socks wet. So, yes, I've followed the party line, taken the necessary steps to becoming a "wild" gardener. Specifically, I've created the requisite number of "wild areas" in the yard: piles of boulders, rotting tree stumps, disorderly growths of blackberry, stinging nettle, couch grass and thistle—all tucked as far out of sight as possible. These unruly pits are intended to serve as refugia for wildlings, snakes and toads and butterfly larvae and God only knows what else. Oases of biodiversity, if the experts are to be believed.

Naturally, I view them with suspicion. They seem to me more like Trojan horses that have breached the garden walls. They crouch in their corners like mangy anarchists plotting their next move against me. Ah, they've got their toehold all right, and maybe the biodiversity crowd imagines there'll soon be a slackening of discipline throughout the whole yard. Naturescapes overrunning the knot garden. Bullfrogs in the reflecting pool. Don't hold your breath. There'll be order in the court if I have anything to say about it. Now, hand me that weed whacker, why don't you, and let's get out there to reassert a bit of control.

Tree Love

DAZZLING AS THE colours of deciduous trees can be in autumn, discerning gardeners know that trees also have supplementary charms. The bark of a certain few, for example, can offer delights, albeit more subtle and intimate, that are every bit as pleasing as vast spectacles of gold and crimson foliage.

The paperbarks prove especially fine when the longer rays of the lowering sun illuminate their scrolls of peeling bark. In our garden, the foliage of a paperbark maple, *Acer griseum,* shows lovely enough autumn colours, blending elements of orange, red and pink; but on a sunny afternoon, its shiny bark exfoliating in translucent rolls of reddish parchment is lit up with a surpassing brilliance. The arbutus tree native to the coast, *Arbutus menziesii,* performs similar magic with its bark. Although its leathery evergreen leaves would win no autumn-colour prizes, the arbutus can sometimes put on a glamorous show of red fruit in the fall, at least until hungry birds show up. Ah, but the bark! Here is a thing of invariably sensuous beauty. Glossy and cinnamon-red, mature bark cracks and peels away in thin strips during the course of summer, exposing a new layer of sometimes startling chartreuse bark beneath. The satin sheen of new bark on the tree's sinuous limbs tempts passing humans not just to look but also touch. To exploring fingertips the surface seems almost carnal in its smooth fleshliness.

This habit of periodically shedding outer bark, as snakes do their skins, is one of several strategies that different trees employ in solving the problem of maintaining a protective sheath around their expanding girth. In temperate regions a great many trees opt to have the cells in the outermost layers of their bark die over time, thereby building up a durable thick skin. As the interior growth rings continue expanding they exert tremendous pressure on the encircling bark, causing it to crack and fissure, often to startling effect. Old oaks are very good at this, their ancient skins forming miniature continents of fracture lines and crevasses. Our native Douglas fir is equally impressive. Oftentimes on a late autumn afternoon we'll permit ourselves a glass of wine while sitting among a stand of maturing Douglas firs to observe how the western sun illuminates the contours of their craggy, reddish-brown bark. On special occasions, one or two brown creepers will alight on the nearby base of a trunk, then creep methodically in an upward spiral, their long tails flattened against the bark while their stiletto bills probe the deep clefts and crevices for insects.

Other trees, including many tropical species, do things differently. Rather than having the outer layers of bark die, they maintain a living bark in which the cells continue to divide, allowing it to stretch and expand as the girth of trunk and limbs increases. The result is a comparatively smooth skin, though perhaps rippled or wrinkled in places, often to appealing effect. The beeches, admirable in so many ways, including autumn colour, are truly outstanding when it comes to sustaining beautifully smooth skin for centuries. The ancient specimens found in the great landscape parks of Britain are heartbreakingly lovely, all smoothness and beguiling sinuosity, trees you can't help but touch and even discreetly hug.

Not long ago, I spent some time on Haida Gwaii and, while stranded in Masset by an apocalyptic storm that sent many of the "No Oil Tankers!" placards whirling down the deserted streets, stayed at a noted B&B named The Copper Beech House, operated by the very fine poet Susan Musgrave. Rather than a headboard, the ground-level bed in which I slept had a large window just beyond which rose the eponymous beech, so that I seemed to fall asleep within the embrace of the big tree's serpentine roots. One could do worse by way of overnight embraces.

We have a copper beech, *Fagus sylvatica* 'Atropurpurea Group', at our place, planted maybe twenty years ago, and it's an abiding source of regret that we will not live to see it as a mature, much less ancient, tree with smoothly rippled skin. Instead we've opted for a shamelessly quick fix in the matter of attractive bark by recently planting a coral bark maple, *Acer palmatum* 'Sango-kaku', in a prominent spot. Although relatively short-lived and sometimes difficult, this is a worthy small tree for all seasons, at no time more so than autumn when its leaves turn to tones of apricot and gold and its distinctive coral-red bark begins to glow more lustrously. By the middle of winter the twigs of the little tree form a burning bush amid the gloom.

So while there's an inevitable and much-mentioned melancholy attached to the falling of autumn leaves, the beauty of bark—whether of beeches or birches or western red cedars—abides for all seasons.

Disquiet in the Forest

OF ALL THE seasons, autumn is the time of trees. Oaks, maples and liquidambars put on their multicoloured cloaks, apple trees hang heavy with fruit, and aspens fashion avenues of gold through interior valleys. Ontario poet Archibald Lampman caught the mood perfectly: "Clothed in splendour, beautifully sad and silent, / Comes the autumn over the woods and highlands, / Golden, rose-red, full of divine remembrance, / Full of foreboding."

Foreboding is certainly on my mind these days, sparked not by the carnival colours of deciduous trees, but by the travails of native conifers. The big Douglas firs, cedars and hemlocks that surround our home and gardens are what first drew us to this piece of land. Though they limit morning and evening sunlight, and terrify us during windstorms, life among the green giants is far preferable to what it would be without them. They are home to innumerable creatures; their dark-green foliage provides a perfect foil for the gardens; and the woodland is a splendid garden in itself. We try our best to blend our transitory plantings into its enduring beauty.

At least, we've always thought of the woodland as enduring. But a few years ago the western hemlocks started to die. Death among juvenile hemlocks is not unusual, as these shade lovers thin themselves out from densely packed stands. But this seemed to be something else. Even young hemlocks colonizing nurse logs on the forest floor—normally storehouses of both nutrients and moisture—were dying in dismal rows. Maturing trees soon followed suit. Designed to live several centuries and reach up to fifty metres in height, they took to drying out and dying over the course of several summers. A scattering of grand firs on our place went the same route. Now we're hearing reports that western red cedars are dying in unprecedented numbers up and down the coast. Skeletons of dead and dying cedars stand like sentinels along Vancouver Island roadways. Several dozen big trees have recently succumbed in our neighbourhood. All summer we've watched tall cedars losing their needles, starting on the topmost branches. What were once dense draperies of green are now exposed limbs dangling listless tassels of foliage. Shallow-rooted and moisture-loving, like the hemlock, cedars appear to also be falling victim to sustained moisture deficits. They are trees of tremendous resilience and may endure, but the signs are ominous.

Many a gardener has been dismayed by dieback in a painstakingly planted cedar hedge; the prospect of dozens of enormous cedars dying around our gardens magnifies that common problem hideously. An iconic life form, growing to tremendous size on prime sites, the underpinning of Native societies along the northwest coast for centuries, *Thuja plicata* is one of earth's great trees. To lose these trees en masse—like losing a run of wild salmon—is to lose a part of ourselves.

Climate change is the likely villain here. Victoria botanist Richard Hebda has warned that "predicted atmospheric change, mainly climate change, will have profound effects on the biodiversity of Canadian forests." Effects may include "the replacement or disappearance of dominant and characteristic species." The devastation wreaked across BC's interior forests by the mountain pine beetle, no longer kept in check by freezing winters, provides testimony to the changes already occurring.

A catalogue of alarming symptoms worldwide is now common currency—rapidly retreating glaciers, warming oceans, melting polar ice. Reports of tempestuous weather have become a staple item on the evening news. Killing droughts, desertification, species extinction—all the symptoms announce to anyone with ears to hear that global climate change is a disaster already under way and one from whose effects none of us will remain immune.

What's a gardener to do? Avoidance is impossible, despair a luxury we can't afford. I've already mentioned that smart gardeners everywhere are already hard at it, installing water catchment and storage systems, fine-tuning their waterwise gardening techniques and deploying in artful ways plants capable of withstanding extreme weather fluctuations.

But, more than that, I've long, and perhaps a touch tiresomely, maintained that gardeners—because we each love a little piece of earth so dearly—are perfectly positioned to champion better treatment of the earth in general. It heartens me to come upon enlightened colleagues who are examining how they live and seeking to reduce or eliminate whatever they can that contributes to the emergency we face. They support community initiatives in the same direction, and hold elected officials accountable, knowing that no politician, no CEO or board of directors, is exempt from addressing this clear and present threat to the well-being of our children and grandchildren. Somebody mentioned to me recently that the current crisis calls for a level of self-sacrifice and social mobilization similar to that achieved during the Second World War. Despite so much evidence to the contrary—whether that be reckless tarsands expansion or airports teeming with frequent flyers—we have to believe our society will eventually prove itself capable of the enormous transition required.

The great British gardener Russell Page wrote: "To plant trees is to give body and life to one's dream of a better world." In a beautifully sad and silent autumn I scan the canopy for dieback, full of foreboding, but knowing that we gardeners and planters of trees cannot, will not, let the dream of a better world die.

Biomimicry

I ENJOYED THE good fortune some time ago of meeting author Janine Benyus, whose book *Biomimicry: Innovation Inspired by Nature* I had found a great read, particularly for gardeners. Biomimicry might sound like another unfortunate fad spawned in the hot tubs of southern California, but in fact it's a science that studies natural designs and processes and applies them to solving human problems. The term, coined by Benyus, derives from the Greek words *bios* (life) and *mimesis* (to imitate).

Nobody strives to imitate nature more ardently than the gardener—our entire undertaking is one long tutelage in how plants function within a complex web of soil nutrients and micro-organisms, climatic conditions, insect pollinators and pests (not to mention the contributions of gardening companions, expert advice-givers and visiting in-laws). Biologists seeking to design superior computing systems by decoding how cells communicate through the lock-and-key jigsawing of enzymes face no stiffer challenge than we do trying to keep our Himalayan blue poppies alive.

As Benyus points out, there's nothing new in using nature as a springboard to innovation—the airplane, telephone and Velcro are among innumerable inventions inspired by natural designs. Two new factors at play today are the need to respond to environmental crisis brought on by carbon binging and the explosive growth of biological knowledge, said to be doubling every five years. We have both the requirement to change our polluting ways and the expanding knowledge base with which to accomplish it.

One of the most intriguing examples Benyus provides is that of natural-systems agriculture as applied to the prairies of the Midwest United States. "For five thousand years," she says, "the prairie has done a great job of holding the soil, resisting pests and weeds, and sponsoring its own fertility, all without our help." In nature's design, the prairie is composed of perennial plants growing in polycultures (many species together) whereas "modern" agriculture sought to replace the prairie with an entirely different system: annual plants grown in monocultures. The consequences have become disastrous—in places, six bushels of plowed topsoil blown away annually for every bushel of corn produced; 160 pounds of chemical fertilizer applied per year for every person in America; vast pesticide-spraying programs. "It works out," she says, "to about ten kilocalories of petroleum to produce one kilocalorie of food. Each year, as the soil becomes poorer and the pests become smarter, our dependence on oil-based inputs escalates."

Some scientists believe the solution to this vicious cycle is to breed perennial food plants that can be grown in a polyculture like the original prairie. Eliminate annual plowing and you eliminate soil erosion. Include nitrogen-fixing perennials in the mix and you reduce dependence upon synthetic fertilizers. A mix of species diffuses the horrendous pest and disease outbreaks of monocultures, eliminating the need for repeated pesticide spraying.

The principle is simplicity itself: Nature's been doing the research and development for millions of years. What works is what we see all around us.

How do you or I set about becoming a biomimetic gardener? Benyus provides a few simple steps she developed from her own experience in trying to renew an aging pond. The first step she calls "quieting human cleverness"—developing an attitude of humility that allows us to acknowledge that nature knows best. Part of this for the gardener may be recognizing the fault lines running through a garden that are sustained by chemical fertilizers and pesticides.

Step two is becoming ecologically literate by listening to nature. Some of this is the work of highly specialized scientists—as Benyus puts it, "We need people who know all there is to know about particular branches of nature's tree." But it also includes the rest of us widening our ecological literacy. In terms of garden problems, we would ask: "What would nature do or not do here? Why or why not?" The answers that nature herself provides to these questions unlock the gate into a garden whose glory lies in its faithfulness to natural processes.

Step three is echoing nature. An engineer seeking to design a desalination system might study the strategies of mangrove trees, which filter sea water through their solar-powered roots. A gardener might carefully analyze the specific growing conditions in various areas of the garden and populate each with plants evolved for that particular condition.

The final step Benyus lists as stewardship. "Once we see nature as a source of inspiration, a mentor, our relationship with the living world changes. We realize that the only way to keep learning from nature is to safeguard naturalness, which is the source of these good ideas."

I very much like the notion of nature as mentor. As Benyus says, "'Doing it nature's way' has the potential to change the way we grow food, make materials, harness energy, heal ourselves, store information and conduct business." And, she might have added, grow splendid natural gardens.

Speaking Volumes

THOUGH BOOKSTORES, BOTH actual and virtual, are awash with glossy, whiz-bang, know-it-all gardening titles packed with pertinent information and gorgeous illustration, during the introspective months of winter I find myself more drawn to musty old volumes that speak of gardening in a world far removed in time and temperament from our own. I pick them up indiscriminately at thrift shops and garage sales and squeeze them onto our crowded shelves, feeling a richer and more well-rounded individual merely for having them in the house.

Nature's Garden by Neltje Blanchan was published in New York in 1900, "With many Color Illustrations." Ms. Blanchan endears herself immediately with the opening sentence of her preface: "Surely a foreword of explanation is called for from one who has the temerity to offer a surfeited public still another book on wild flowers." If the public was surfeited a century ago, it must be positively bloated today. Subtitled *An aid to our knowledge of our wild flowers and their insect visitors,* the book catalogues over five hundred North American wildflowers, grouped by flower colour, with meticulous descriptions of plant parts, preferred habitat, flowering season, distribution and the individual ability of each plant to attract pollinators. Blanchan writes: "Thus it is to the night-flying moth, long of tongue, keen of scent, that we are indebted for the deep, white, fragrant Easter lily, for example, and not to the florist; albeit the moth is in his turn indebted to the lily for the length of his tongue and his keen nerves: neither could have advanced without the other. What long vistas through the ages of creation does not this inter-dependence of flowers and insects open!" Rich with allusions from science, folklore and romantic poetry—while discussing creeping wintergreen, *Gaultheria procumbens,* the author quotes Bryant: "Where cornels arch their cool dark boughs o'er beds of wintergreen"—this is garden writing of antique appeal more than a century later.

The Book of Perennials by Alfred C. Hottes was first published in 1923 in New York, bearing the disclaimer "This book makes no pretext as to botanical precision"—a precaution certain contemporary writers might do well to consider. The slender volume attempts "to present only the most outstanding perennials, flowers which are either so strong that they almost care for themselves, or so exquisitely charming that they warrant any amount of time in rearing them properly."

The chapter on "Insects and Diseases" provides insight into control measures employed before the pesticide revolution following the Second World War. For controlling cutworms, for example, the reader is advised to "Mix about a teaspoon of arsenate of lead, a tablespoon of molasses and a little water to each handful of wheat bran. Place a tablespoon here and there about the garden just before dark to kill cutworms. There is no danger of killing birds with the bran if it is placed under a shingle or a piece of wood where they cannot reach it." A concentrated form of nicotine extract is described as "death to the Rose lice or any other lice or sucking insects." For fungicides, gardeners were instructed to rely on Flowers of Sulphur, Bordeaux Mixture and Ammoniacal Copper Sulphate, all of which, if nothing else, had more elegant names than contemporary chemicals.

Hottes was obviously a list person, as one idiosyncratic chapter is titled "The Lists of Twenty-Fives," including "Twenty-Five Tallest Plants," "Twenty-Five Most Used White Perennials for Garden Effect," and "Twenty-Five Daisy-like Flowers of Various Colors." There is none of today's fixation on the latest this and the newest that. Rather, Hottes writes, "It is a compliment to a flower to call it 'old-fashioned,' for that indicates that the flower was popular with our grandparents and was so worthwhile that we grow them even today." A particular charm of this, and many other old gardening books, is the use of black-and-white photographs and line drawings. They have an antique loveliness and tranquillity about them that is inherent in the attraction of gardening itself.

Something of the same holds true for a third small volume titled *Garden Manures and Fertilisers*, written by R.P. Faulkner in Nottingham, England, in 1949. Amid very serious discussions of the merits of farmyard manure, hoof and horn meal, wool shoddy and steamed bone flower, there are classic old black-and-white photos. One shows a vigorous-looking young countrywoman piling up vegetable matter and manure in an enormous compost heap. Others picture old duffers in gumboots, suit jackets and cloth caps "working lawn mowings into the bottom of the runner-bean trench," and "applying a winter dressing of potash in the form of wood ashes." All very scientifically controlled activities, of course, and no room for nonsense, for as Faulkner warns: "If one admits the existence of a factor in plant nutrition which does not conform to the ascertained facts then, in effect, one may as well intone a chant over a starving plant while pouring over it water from the trunk of a hollow tree taken at midnight at the time of the full moon!" Ouch.

Antiquated and overblown as they may be in places, still many old books of this type speak to at least some gardeners of the twenty-first century in a time-honoured way that much of the "Hot! Hot! Hottest New Hybrids!" hyperbole never can.

Always Living

DURING THE MURK of winter it's salutary to have some plants about the place that are exemplars of survival despite hard times. Sempervivums are a genus with just this particular genius. They may be familiarly called houseleeks, or hens and chicks, but in the time of darkness it's better to stick with their formal name, *Sempervivum,* meaning "always living." It is these little fellows' lust for life, their cheerfulness amid harsh and dispiriting conditions, that especially endears them to us. We may have endured a fortnight of relentless rain or a cold snap that has sapped the spirit from most of the garden, leaving desiccated skeletons rattling in the wind. Never mind. The feisty little rosettes of sempervivums still have enough life in them to recolonize the planet if required.

Although almost tropical in appearance, like echeverias or aeoniums, they're actually mountain dwellers, surviving in the wild up to twenty-five hundred metres above sea level. Their native haunts, scattered from Morocco to Iran, include some of the most fabled ranges on earth: the peaks of Iberia and Armenia, the Alps, the Carpathian, Caucasus and Balkan Mountains. The storied homelands of the sempervivum read like an alpine enthusiast's dream expedition. And, believe me, the number of "semp lovers" is legion. There are only about forty or so species in the genus, but thanks to the ministrations of enthusiasts there are several thousand named cultivars, many of which offer such infinitesimally minute variations in the form or colour of their foliage as to be indistinguishable from one another to anyone other than a sempermaniac.

The rosettes can come in strong reds and pinks, through orange, yellow, brown and green, but in shady conditions all may fade toward a uniform green. Other variations in growth conditions can cause changes in the plant's appearance, making identification difficult. Being severely taxonomically challenged myself, I prefer to gaze fondly upon our houseleeks and not worry myself about their names. Nevertheless, a few years ago we found ourselves the beneficiary of a choice collection of sempervivums, a generous gift from Jim Rollerson on the Sunshine Coast. This wonderful selection of unusual species, including types of the intriguing cobweb houseleek, *S. arachnoideum,* whose white fibres resemble a spiderweb, came originally from his mother's garden. The late Grace Rollerson was a renowned succulent enthusiast, and her collection can now be viewed in the alpine garden at the University of British Columbia Botanical Garden.

Whether you've got a prized collection or only a few species, there's much to admire in sempervivums. For starters, they'll flourish almost any place where there's a thimbleful of gritty soil to get a toehold in. We have them hanging out of rock walls and tucked into crevices along stone pathways, as well as on the sod roof. And they grow wonderfully in those big clay strawberry planters, where different varieties can occupy separate pockets and not overrun one another.

Although small and entirely undemanding, at heart these are rebels come down from wild mountains and not beholden to anyone. The trick to their toughness lies in their thick leaves that can store water against long periods of drought, allowing them to tolerate a baking summer sun. And they'll shrug off a deep freeze equally well. You never have to ask, "I wonder if the houseleeks made it through that last dreadful spell?"

They are, as well, profoundly communal plants, typically found packed together in colonies. This is a result of their propagation strategies. When an individual plant produces a flowering stem—and the tiny, star-like flowers are exquisite—it self-pollinates. After flowering for the first and only time, the plant dies, but is succeeded by an extended family of rosettes formed as lateral offsets. The individual doesn't "live forever," but the colony does, offering a handsome reflection on mortality and collectivity.

I also appreciate their long history as a medicinal and witch-plant, and the fact that they were commonly grown on roofs as protection against lightning strikes and sorcery. But it is that "always living" aspect that appeals most surely. The longer I stay at this gardening racket, the more I come to fully appreciate that it is at its core a fantastically elaborate form of life celebration. As human foolhardiness in destroying the natural world accelerates, so does thinking individuals' appreciation of all life forms, whether in the garden or in the wild. It's for that very reason I believe we gardeners belong rightfully among the foremost champions of all living things as precious and irreplaceable. Huddled in the depths of winter, the "always living" sempervivum gives us hope for brighter days ahead.

Wisdom of the Aged

IT'S FUNDAMENTALLY UNACCEPTABLE that gardeners should grow old. We are, after all, people oozing with rebirth and renewal, keenly alert to the seasonal possibilities of fresh growth. In the current idiom: We're all about life. And talk about a healthy lifestyle!...habitually outdoors, engaged in more rigorous exercise than a world-class triathlete, fuelled by a cornucopia of fresh organic fruits and vegetables of our own cultivation.

And yet we grow old. One no longer bounds outdoors seething with energy for the tasks at hand. For some it's more like the slow and solemn trudge of a funeral cortege. And the work—oh, the work! Stones, pots, buckets of soil and the like all seem unaccountably bulkier than they once did. Everything's a few steps farther away than it used to be, as though space begins to stretch as time continues to shrink. Fingers that once could nimbly pluck weeds from the earth for hours now grope clumsily and painfully. Knees go. Hips go. The lower back tightens up. Shoulders freeze. Tendonitis bites at wrists and elbows. "Lock down" pertains less to what the cops do at a crime scene than to what the gardener's body does when it's gotten into some idiotic contortion that can't be gotten out of. Ascending the orchard ladder to pick a few apples takes on heroic dimensions while triggering unwelcome recollection of how many acquaintances over the years have suffered crippling or even fatal falls from ladders.

Nevertheless, there can be no question of retirement. Not while the peonies need their cages or the carrots require thinning. But there does periodically occur a time for rational reassessment of one's circumstances. Winter is good for this, when the siren calls of the soil are sufficiently muted for common sense to get a few words in.

Is the place really getting to be too much?

Possibly so. But sometimes things are as much in the head as in the hedge. Perhaps an attitudinal change is in order. To begin with, for example, consider the tyranny of perfectionism. The need to have everything just so, all of the time, as though a tour bus full of master gardeners is about to descend on the place and render harsh judgment. In reality, there is no requirement that the garden be perfect, except in the gardener's own mind. Yes, of course, you've worked like a slave all these years to achieve something very special. And you have. But perfection in the garden, like purity of heart, is an elusive goal, mercurial and impermanently attainable. If the garden starts becoming more burden than pleasure, does it not make sense to consider nuancing the ideal a touch? After all, letting go of a mental construct is vastly less painful than abandoning a beloved garden. The aging gardener is under no obligation to maintain a perfectionist show garden for the approval of anyone, including oneself. So let it be a bit unkempt here and there, intolerable as that might have seemed a decade ago. Celebrate its frowzy state, feeling emancipatory delight in its wanton beauty rather than anxiety that it isn't behaving itself.

On a more practical level, there is the consideration of getting in help, and blessed indeed are those with vigorous young relatives or friends reliably able to lend a hand. Hired help too is a grand thing for those able to afford it and to secure it in these uncertain times.

Otherwise, one needs to begin eliminating, or at least reducing, the high-maintenance stuff. Enormous rambling roses, rapturous as they can be when blooming, entail a certain level of vigorous push-back if they're not to overrun the place. As with long-held grudges, perhaps the time for thorny battles is drawing to an end. Similarly, plants that require endless pruning, staking, shearing, cutting down and carting off may need to give way to less demanding specimens. Or deployment strategies can shift a bit. Certain vines, for example, rather than being painstakingly attached to obelisks and lattices every year, might simply be left to sprawl across nearby shrubs where they're far easier to deal with.

As for the gardening work itself, a wise old gardener years ago told me that the trick is not to do any one thing for too long. Rather than weeding for hours, instead tackle a succession of different jobs, each of which involves fresh positioning and activity. It's amazing, too, to discover how many tasks that used to require stooping and bending can be done from a sitting or kneeling position, although getting up from sitting and kneeling positions isn't quite the fluid bound it used to be. By all means, take more breaks than were previously permitted. How marvellous, after all those years of brisk efficiency, to now allow oneself the luxury of regularly stopping work and simply being in the garden for a while, entirely free from guilt and anxiety.

I detect an increasing emphasis nowadays on doing warm-up exercises before starting garden work, followed by cool-down exercises after concluding it. Let's be honest: this cuts against the grain of the gnarly gardener. Imagine taking time for a bout of knee bends and spinal flexing instead of getting on with things. But if that's what's required in the end, so be it.

The whole point is one doesn't want the garden to become an object of resentment or worry. Old age itself can hold enough of both. Rather it should, insofar as possible, be a source of continued joy, as well as sweet remembrance even as twilight descends.

Most important of all, it seems to me, is to sustain an attitude of thankfulness that one has spent at least a portion of one's life within the enchantments of gardening. This is a great benefice to have received: a personal small sampling of paradise, as well as a singular contribution to re-creating the beauty and bounty of our garden-like planet. A blessing both received and given. A celebration of life and a revolution of hope in which we've played some small part. The dream of a world at peace in which none go hungry and all are free to roam through loveliness.

INDEX